SPIRITUALLY ABLE

Other Works by David Rizzo and Mercedes McBride Rizzo

Adaptive First Eucharist Preparation Kit

My Picture Missal and iPad App

Other Books by David Rizzo

Faith, Family, and Children with Special Needs: How Catholic Parents and Their Kids with Special Needs Can Develop a Richer Spiritual Life

SPIRITUALLY ABLE

A Parent's Guide to Teaching the Faith to Children with Special Needs

By
DAVID RIZZO
AND
MERCEDES McBRIDE RIZZO

LOYOLAPRESS.
A JESUIT MINISTRY
Chicago

LOYOLA PRESS.
A JESUIT MINISTRY

3441 N. Ashland Avenue
Chicago, Illinois 60657
(800) 621-1008
www.loyolapress.com

Cover art credit: Texture art, Foxtrot101/iStock/Thinkstock, chalice and host, Loyola Press.

ISBN-13: 978-0-8294-4207-6
ISBN-10: 0-8294-4207-3
Library of Congress Control Number: 2014953015

Printed in the United States of America.

14 15 16 17 18 19 20 Versa 10 9 8 7 6 5 4 3 2 1

To our children,
Brendan, Colin, Danielle, and Shannon,
for all that you have taught us.
May you continue to inspire others.
May you follow your dreams.

To our parents,
John and Mary Elizabeth McBride
"Ar dheis Dé go raibh siad"
(May They Rest In Peace)
and
Vincent and Ellen Rizzo
"Our Vines Have Tender Grapes"

Faith is taking the first step even when you don't see the whole staircase.
—Martin Luther King Jr.

Danielle Rizzo's First Holy Communion, August 5, 2006.

Contents

Preface

When we were married more than twenty years ago, we never thought we would be raising a child with special needs. During our pre-Cana classes, the presenter asked us to consider several possible parenting scenarios. These included infertility, adoption, and raising a child with a disability. We were open to each of these possibilities at some level, but we were sure such circumstances would never apply to us. About ten years later, we did face one of these scenarios when we learned that our third child—our daughter Danielle—had autism. For some time after we learned this, we did not comprehend the magnitude of it and what it would actually mean for our family.

Eventually, we discovered that we were not the only couple being called to raise a child with special needs. Many other parents are on the same journey. It takes faith to raise any child, but this is especially true when the child has a disability. The very experience of loving a child with special needs can motivate you to look inward, deepen your own faith, and pass on that faith to others, especially to the child.

This book is about how parents can teach the Catholic faith to the very special child that God has given them. When a child has autism or another disability, creative approaches are often needed to maximize learning. When Danielle was ready to begin learning about God, we knew that her religious education would be different from that of her brothers because it would have to be modified to match her abilities, learning style, and cognitive needs. We knew that we would have to partner with the parish religious education program, and we found ourselves becoming much more active in the process. This was difficult at times but also exhilarating. It wasn't long before we began to see that we were being called to a ministry.

In this book we share what we have learned as a couple about educating a child with a serious disability in the Catholic faith. The content is designed to support what local catechists and directors of religious education (DREs) are doing. Each chapter centers on particular religious concepts, introduced by a story from our experience. The techniques and approaches we present are similar to what has been shown to be effective in special education generally.

Teaching at Home

Nearly all religious education programs have an at-home dimension. The at-home setting becomes extremely important when teaching children with special needs. While the local parish is responsible for the overall management of your child's religious education program, to ensure that all necessary and relevant content is taught, you the parent will be instrumental in helping them individualize this instruction in a way that will make the Catholic faith come alive for your child.

There are many advantages to working at home with children with special needs. Working in the home can supplement what goes on in the parish classroom. When we took Danielle at age five to a neighboring parish to participate in its classroom-based special needs program, we found that she responded well to much of the program. However, she needed more one-to-one attention due to her severe language deficits and high activity level. We give kudos to the parish and its special needs ministry volunteers for their foresight and dedication. They developed a great program where all are truly welcome and no child is turned away. In fact, several families traveled many miles for the opportunity to be educated in the Catholic faith there. We were grateful to have found this program, but we also decided to work with a special needs catechist from our own parish, who was able to provide one-to-one instruction in our home.

At-home instruction from our parish catechist allowed all our children to make their sacraments in the same parish, something that was important to us as a family. Danielle was already attending a different school than her brothers and sister. She was participating in Special Olympics, while her siblings participated in the township recreation program. Because just about everything else she was going through seemed to distance her from our family, we wanted her to be part of our parish. And the logistics of trying to keep up with the demands of two separate religious education programs in two separate towns, with four children between the ages of two and ten, were simply too much. There were times when we were dashing from one parish to the other at rush hour with Danielle and her two-year-old sister in tow, hoping that we would arrive in time to pick up our sons from their program before it ended.

We found that working in the home had many other practical advantages. We were able to provide one-on-one instruction, better control over the time of day, and ready access to highly preferred items for reinforcement such as her favorite TV shows, video games, backyard swings, songs, and snacks. We could deliver these more easily at appropriate times and frequencies during a home session. The number of concepts presented, the frequency and duration of breaks, and what constitutes appropriate reinforcement can be customized to fit the needs and abilities of each child. Children differ, but we found that a good rule for Danielle was no more than one or two concepts presented per lesson, with frequent breaks. Also, the familiarity of home is comforting to children who often have difficulty in unfamiliar surroundings and circumstances, and who learn best with routine and predictability. The familiar setting gives the child a sense of control and security. Certainly, this was true for Danielle.

Reinforcement and Prompts

Parents of very young children with special needs can be overwhelmed by the demands of teaching their children. There is so much to learn and, like many parents, we had to educate ourselves. We did, however, have some advantages in this area. David is a physical therapist who works with people with disabilities on a daily basis. He has access to the latest scientific literature on autism and brain development, particularly how it relates to the development of learning strategies. As a teacher, Mercedes has worked with children who have individualized education plans (IEPs) and was familiar with the need for educational accommodation. Our background and experience helped us understand and adapt special education techniques such as reinforcement and prompting.

Providing reinforcement for correct responses is an effective tool when teaching any child, but it is especially effective for those with special needs. This is often the best way to connect with the child early in the learning process, especially if he or she lacks the cognitive and language skills for other types of learning. Reinforcement learning works this way: when a child gives the response you are looking for, the child receives an item or activity that he or she likes. An example would be a highly preferred item. Some children may do well receiving verbal praise or perhaps small food items such as a cracker or mint. Others may prefer sensory input such as receiving deep-pressure, playing on the swings, or taking a short break. (Deep pressure is the application of a tactile stimulus to provide the feeling of a firm hug, holding, swaddling, or massage.) Fortunately, parents tend to be familiar with their child's preferred reinforcements. When we were beginning to work with Danielle, we needed to experiment with different reinforcements before we found the ones that worked best for her. She responded particularly well to food items such as cheese curls and Goldfish crackers.

When teaching a new skill, you may need to provide prompts to facilitate learning. There are several types of prompts, including hand-over-hand and other physical prompts, visual prompts, and verbal prompts. A hand-over-hand prompt is when you place your hand over the child's hand and gently guide it to make the correct response—for instance, pointing to a picture or choosing from a set of objects. Other physical prompts can be used to gently move the child's whole body, such as moving from sitting to standing. Visual prompts include gestures and pictures. Children with autism and other disabilities often rely on visual information. An example of a gestural prompt we used with Danielle was to point at an object to show her that it was the correct answer. A picture prompt is using a visual schedule or displaying pictures in sequence to show the steps in an activity or task.

Prompts are used in the early stages of teaching a new skill and should be discontinued when they are no longer needed to get the correct response. The objective is to get the child to make the correct response so that you can provide the reinforcement. Reinforcement leads to learning the skill. Reinforcement is used less frequently and phased out altogether when the child makes the correct response without help.

Games and Puzzles

When you have a child who is very limited in terms of vocabulary and reading skills, it is sometimes best to introduce concepts using a different approach than the traditional book or lecture. Games and puzzles are effective because they are visual and interactive. There are games modeled on favorite childhood games, such as Candy Land and Old Maid, but with religious content. The *Adaptive First Eucharist Preparation Kit* and the other sacramental preparation kits published by Loyola Press include puzzles, social stories, and icons. In addition, the *Adaptive Finding God Program* includes puzzles, picture cards, and a picture glossary of catechetical terms. We refer to specific items when appropriate. You can customize your own games, puzzles, and cards, using images familiar and pleasing to your child. For Danielle, we found we could make homemade games and puzzles using easily obtainable materials such as laminated note cards, and we made a simple puzzle about going to Mass. Puzzles can be useful tools for children because they enjoy the feeling of flipping and manipulating the pieces. Some children will be able to play these games by themselves while others will need prompting or some assistance. Danielle needed us to provide assistance. Familiarity is effective, and repetition is key.

Connect to the Word

Hear, O Israel: The LORD is our God, the LORD alone. You shall love the LORD your God with all your heart, and with all your soul, and with all your might. Keep these words that I am commanding you today in your heart. Recite them to your children and talk about them when you are at home and when you are away, when you lie down and when you rise. Bind them as a sign on your hand, fix them as an emblem on your forehead, and write them on the doorposts of your house and on your gates.

—Deuteronomy 6:4–9

How to Use This Book

Parents and religious educators can use this book in several ways. You can read this book straight through or in any order, depending on where your child is relative to his or her religious formation and the needs of your family. Some chapters deal with sacramental preparation. These chapters provide an opportunity for your family to supplement and support what your parish catechist is doing. However, other chapters pertain to more topical issues such as Christian service, family celebrations, and dealing with grief and loss. Parents can use these chapters at any time that is deemed appropriate and return to them as often as needed.

Each chapter focuses on a religious theme or sacrament and opens with a story from our lives that sets the stage for the lessons that follow. It is our hope that parents can relate to these stories and find humor and hope in our struggles and how we learned to manage the challenges we faced as a family of a child with special needs. As mentioned earlier, each chapter includes two or three lessons that can help you introduce your child to the Catholic faith and provide the skills he or she needs to prepare successfully for the sacraments, attend and focus in Mass, and learn about God and his people, including how we recognize and celebrate the God who dwells among us. Typically, each lesson begins with "For Starters," an introductory activity that the family can do at home. "The Fun Begins" describes a game or other play-oriented activity that gets your child thinking and moving toward applying what he or she has learned. Next, the focus of the lesson, "Making It Real," turns to integrating what has been learned in the home and family to the outside community both at church and in the secular world. Each lesson ends with "Connect to the Word," a Scripture passage that provides inspiration and an opportunity to expose your child to the Bible at a level he or she can understand. Each chapter concludes with "A Closing Meditation," a quotation that allows parents to explore their faith in a deeper way.

1

Familiarizing Your Child with the Church

Our pastor, Father Phil, likes to say, "Parents are the first teachers of their children." This truth can be very rewarding and a bit frightening. One of our earliest memories of teaching the faith to our children is nightly bedtime reading from a children's Bible. These were wonderful moments, and you could see it in the children's faces, in their expressions of wonder at the amazing things God had done. This was their first exposure to great stories such as Noah's ark, Adam and Eve, and the parables of Jesus. These were wonderful moments for us as well, as we relived the awe and excitement we felt the first time we heard these stories.

There were so many religious lessons to pass on to our children when they were younger. We told them about God and how much he loved them. We explained about right and wrong and the importance of loving God and neighbor. We explained about guardian angels and how they would keep watch over you and protect you from harm. On Sundays we brought our children to church. At that time, Baptisms, First Holy Communions, and weddings were a common occurrence on both sides of our large family. These events provided natural opportunities to expose our children to the sacraments.

When our boys reached an appropriate age, we enrolled them in formal religious education. They received their First Holy Communion preparation at our church. We signed them up with ease, never questioning for a moment whether or not they would be accepted into our parish religious education program. They went through the program without a hitch and satisfied the requirements for First Holy Communion without difficulty. All this time, we were unaware that there were other children for whom sacramental preparation would not be so easy. We had no idea that the process can be a challenging experience for children with disabilities or that very few parishes had special needs programs.

None of that was on our radar yet and wouldn't be until after Danielle's autism was diagnosed. Raising a family was still new to us. Like other young parents, we were quite green and still finding our way. So much of parenting is learned by muddling through and making mistakes. This may be why older siblings never tire from complaining about how much stricter their parents were for the older children and how lenient for the younger. Nobody gives you a handbook when you become a new parent.

When our boys were very young, we sometimes needed to use the crying room during Mass. Many churches have a small quiet room set aside for families of young children. While the room's large window allows you to see and hear the Mass, the other parishioners are spared from hearing crying babies and noisy toddlers.

We often shared the crying room with a young mother who attended church every week with her four children. None of them appeared to be older than five. Her two littlest ones sat in a long double stroller while the two older boys took over the room. We were no strangers to rambunctious boys—that's why we were in the crying room in the first place. However, to say that her boys were swinging from chandeliers wouldn't have been much of an exaggeration.

The room was a dual-purpose room. In addition to being used by parents as a crying room during Mass, it was the storage room for priest vestments and other items. The neatly pressed and immaculate clerical garb hung on hangers in the room as if in a museum. While the rest of us kept our distance out of fear and trembling, this woman's boys would literally climb the rack that held the vestments. On more than one occasion, we had to intervene to prevent the heavily laden rack from falling over. During the car ride home, we often discussed what we viewed as her poor parenting skills.

Looking back now, it is very clear that we were unfairly judgmental about her parenting skills. This young woman was very devout. Week after week she brought her children to Mass by herself. She seemed overwhelmed and frazzled. We were harsh and misguided in our assessment of the situation. We realize now that at least one of her boys had a cognitive or behavioral disability. Little did we know that this experience in the crying room was providing us a glimpse into our own future.

Danielle's autism has been our greatest challenge in life, but it has also been one of our greatest blessings. It has led us down a path we never dreamed of taking and would never have chosen. It has tested our faith and strengthened it, and it has taught us to trust God even when things turn out far different from what we expected.

We learned other things too, but all in good time. For one thing, we learned humility and mercy. We learned that parents of children with disabilities are doing the best they can in difficult situations. That is why we want to promote greater awareness about the challenges for children with special needs who attend Mass. We have learned that things may not always be as simple as they seem and that we ought not be so quick to judge people's parenting skills or apparent lack of discipline. Few people outside the community of children with special needs and their families understand how much of a challenge it can be.

One of the most important ways that parents can rise to the challenge is by educating their children about church, what happens there, and how to behave in an appropriate and reverent manner. When we did this with Danielle, we saw a real improvement in her behavior. This was a gradual process with ups and downs, but over time we have seen real growth in her ability to attend and focus at Mass. She has learned to follow along and act appropriately. The following lessons will give parents the tools they need to succeed at this inspired task.

Lesson 1: Introducing Your Child to Church

An easy place to start is to introduce the concept of "What is a church?" Children with disabilities have probably been in church, especially if they have older siblings, but they may have no idea why it is important or that it is God's house.

For Starters

Take pictures of your church using your cell phone or a digital camera. You can print these or show them directly from the device. The latter is an excellent option if your child uses an iPad or electronic tablet. Danielle responded best to laminated pictures that she could point to, match, and physically manipulate. However, some children will prefer to use an electronic device.

Show a picture of your church to your child. Use a hand-over-hand prompt for the child to touch the picture. Explain that this is a church and that people go there to spend time with God. In the same way, have your child point to the features of the church building, such as the steeple. Show a picture of the interior. Show the altar, baptismal font, pews, and so on. Be sure that you say the name of each feature as you perform the hand-over-hand prompts.

If the child can speak or communicate in other ways, ask the child to name the people who live in his or her house. If necessary, use a verbal prompt: "Mommy and Daddy, sister, brother." Explain to your child that the church is God's house and that God lives there.

The Fun Begins

An easy place to start is to introduce the concept of "What is a church and how do we behave there?" One great way is to use a plush church set, often available for purchase at religious supply stores. Such sets are similar to a doll house but represent a church and are made of soft cloth. A typical set comes with church pews, altar, and figurines, including a priest and parishioners. Danielle had been in church many times before, but using the plush set allowed her to focus on specific features of the church and become acquainted with these in an orderly way. You might also consider role-play or stick puppets; Loyola Press offers a set of stick puppets with a church interior backdrop.

Sit with your child in front of the set. Point out that this is a church and that a church is God's house. Show him or her the steeple, the altar, and the doors. If your child can engage in imaginary play, he or she can pretend that he or she is at church. Have your child manipulate the priest figurine or puppet or pretend that one of the figurines or puppets is playing the organ. Explain that they are singing to God.

Ask, "Who is the priest?" Then allow the child to pick up the priest figurine. If needed, provide a hand-over-hand prompt by gently placing your own hand over the child's hand and guiding it to the figurine. Talk about the special clothing the priest wears and tell about how church is a special place. It is where we go on the weekend for Mass. Because it is so special, we need to behave in a special way. That means being extra quiet, staying in our seats, and paying attention. This approach works best for children who are verbal, with good receptive language skills, meaning that they can comprehend language heard or read and can respond well to questions. There is a large variation in what each child can comprehend. Some children do not understand imaginative play. However, they can learn in other ways, such as matching picture to picture or using a social story.

Making It Real

Once the child understands the concept of church, you can expand on it by walking around the grounds of your church and pointing to some of the same features you discussed with the pictures, the plush set, or the stick puppets, such as stained-glass windows and the steeple. Now go inside your church. Point out the altar, baptismal font, organ, and even the restrooms. All of this makes the church more familiar to your child. We found that it was a good idea to take Danielle to our church during quiet times when Mass was not going on. We would stop for a brief visit, sit in the pew, kneel on the kneelers, genuflect, and bless ourselves. Then we would practice sitting quietly, for a few moments at first and then building up to longer sessions as she was able. Even when Danielle had trouble staying calm and quiet, it was okay because the church was empty. This practice gave Danielle an opportunity to learn, and it gave us a peaceful refuge in the middle of our day when we needed it most.

Another way to teach children about church is by using a toy Noah's ark. Noah's ark can be a metaphor for the church as a place to gather and worship God. Noah's ark toy sets are readily available. The tangibility of the toy set allows your child to feel the weight of the ark and the shapes of the animals. He or she can manipulate the figures of Noah, Noah's wife, and the animals. However, we recommend that these pieces be unbreakable and small enough for a child to hold safely. Because most children love a good story, introduce the story using a children's Bible. Some children's Bibles have very few words or no words but lots of pictures. Danielle responds well to a Bible that has virtually no text. The pages are filled with large and colorful illustrations. A picture Bible allows you to tell the story and build on the child's knowledge base, and it gives you the freedom to tell the story in any way that connects with your child. Even today, Danielle has difficulty paying attention to books and stories. This difficulty was even more pronounced when she was younger. Although her ability to sit for stories was limited, we would point to the pictures. She liked the pictures of the animals on the ark. Sometimes she would smile and point when we provided a hand-over-hand or gestural prompt. Sometimes she would laugh or babble. Another picture she enjoyed was of Eve biting into the apple in the Garden of Eden. So try telling Bible stories using a picture Bible. Afterward, bring out the toy ark and animals and role-play with your child.

Connect to the Word

As for me, I am establishing my covenant with you and your descendants after you, and with every living creature that is with you, the birds, the domestic animals, and every animal of the earth with you, as many as came out of the ark.

—Genesis 9:9–10

Tell your child that God is with us in church and always. Know that yourself as well.

Emphasize that Noah and the animals in the ark know and love God. Explain that people in church know and love God too.

Lesson 2: Reverent Behavior in Church

Children with disabilities may have no idea that church is a special place that calls for a certain type of behavior that is different from behavior at home. Noise volume, freedom of movement, talking, and where to place attention are all more restricted at church.

For Starters

Catholics do several things to show reverence in church. When we enter the church, we bless ourselves with holy water. We listen reverently, and we pray. You can practice these behaviors at home with your child.

There are special containers for holy water, as well as holy water fonts that can hang on your wall. These can be purchased online and at religious supply stores. You can go to church and fill the container with holy water and bring it back to your house for use in this lesson and as a daily devotional if desired. In our home, we have a beautiful holy water font that shows the Holy Family. It was given to us by Mercedes's father, Poppy. There was always a holy water font in her childhood home, and when our children were small and we visited Poppy, he would lift them up to dip their fingers into the font. He wanted his grandchildren to continue that tradition in their own home. The font is especially meaningful to our children now that Poppy is no longer with us.

Stand with your child in front of the holy water font. Gently place your hand over the child's, and using a hand-over-hand prompt, show him or her how to dip his or her hand into the water without splashing. Make the Sign of the Cross. You may find that your child is resistant to the coldness or wetness of the water. If this is a problem, just dip the tip of the finger into the water. When you do this, you can say aloud the words, "In the name of the Father, and of the Son, and of the Holy Spirit. Amen." Encourage your child to repeat these words if he or she is able. Try doing this several times, as repetition helps with learning. Provide reinforcement with a preferred item or activity. At some point, see if the child can perform this blessing without the prompt. Progress may be slow at first, but with repetition you will see greater and greater success. Danielle loved to try to splash at first, but we were able to prevent this with the hand-over-hand prompt. It took a long time to phase out this prompt, but now she has learned to use holy water properly without splashing.

Some children have difficulty with hand-over-hand prompts for various reasons. If that is the case, use a visual prompt instead. Dip your hand in the font and bless yourself. Ask the child to do what you do. Often he or she will imitate the action that was modeled. In some cases, the child may have trouble imitating you in mirror fashion. If so, sit or stand next to your child and face the same direction he or she is facing. Make sure he or she can still see what you are doing and visually model the blessing.

The Fun Begins

Another way to show reverence is to sit with hands folded in prayer. At home there are several natural occasions during the day when you can teach your child how to pray. Two good times are at meals and before bed. At dinnertime make it a habit for the family to say grace together. Any short prayer will do, from a beautiful, simple prayer such as the Sign of the Cross to something more elaborate like the Grace Before Meals:

> Bless us, O Lord, and these thy gifts, which we are about to receive from thy bounty, through Christ our Lord. Amen.

It is important that the prayer be the same each time. Your child will soon begin to pick it up naturally due to the strong reinforcement of eating afterward. A nonverbal child would not be expected to say the prayer, but he or she can learn to sit reverently with hands folded and make the Sign of the Cross or an approximation of it. We find it heartwarming to see our nonverbal daughter immediately join in when our family begins to say grace. She does this by waiting with her hands pressed together to eat and making the Sign of the Cross before and after the rest of us say the prayer out loud. Sometimes she will attempt to pronounce the words. This is called a verbal approximation.

Bedtime prayers are trickier. We've found the best way to handle prayer at bedtime is to keep it simple and make it a habit. You might try leading your child in the following prayer: "Dear God, thank you for this day." If your child is more verbal, you might select a standard prayer such as the Hail Mary or the Lord's Prayer. Visually model how to fold hands in prayer and reinforce when the child does this successfully.

Making It Real

Now it's time to take your child to church for a practice run. Do this at a time when the church is quiet and a Mass is not going on. During this time, you and your child can practice sitting in the pew and using the kneeler. Show your child how to genuflect when entering the pew. You can use a gentle physical prompt along with visual modeling.

When you do attend Mass, seat selection is critical. Consider attending the least crowded Mass so that plenty of seats will be available. Factors to consider in seat selection include proximity to the organ and choir and having sufficient space between your child and those around you. Some children enjoy being near the music, while others find it hard to tolerate the volume. Some children have difficulty when the pew is too crowded. You may want to experiment to see which works best. We did this by trial and error, watching Danielle's reactions, noticing for instance if she covered her ears. We gauged it the best we could from how well she sat for Mass on any given day. We ended up on the side near where the altar servers sat. This worked well when our daughter

Shannon later became an altar server. We arrived early each week and sat in approximately the same pew each time, which helped establish a routine that Danielle found comforting. Also, we placed Danielle between the two of us so either could help her when needed.

The *My Picture Missal* flip book, which we authored and is available through Loyola Press, is an excellent resource for your child at Mass. Children may not know what they are expected to be doing at any given time, and they may have difficulty understanding what is going on during the Mass. The *My Picture Missal* flip book has two pictures on each page. The first shows the position of the child's body: standing, sitting, or kneeling. The second picture shows what is happening: the readings, sign of peace, collection basket, and the other parts of Mass.

Parents can guide their child in using the missal by doing the following:

- Hold the missal open to the correct page. Use hand-over-hand prompts to show your child the picture of the correct body position. If he or she moves into the correct position on his or her own, reinforce him or her for doing so. If not, use a physical prompt to gently guide him or her into the correct position and then provide reinforcement.

- Provide a hand-over-hand prompt to point out the picture of what is happening at this moment in the Mass. Praise your child when he or she shows interest, looks up at the altar, or shows that he or she is oriented to that part of the Mass in some way.

- Turn the page when appropriate or prompt the child to do this. At some point, test if he or she can hold the missal by himself or herself. Continue to provide any prompts or support needed for your child to be successful with the missal and continue to provide reinforcement.

Until recently, one of us would hold the missal and turn the pages for Danielle. A few months ago, she began to hold the missal by herself and flip the page when one of us pointed to the missal. She is gradually learning to be more independent with this activity. We trust that one day she will follow along all by herself. Also, we use the missal's picture exchange cards to help her stay focused. Sometimes Danielle uses the new *My Picture Missal* app at Mass. For children who prefer electronic devices, this is an excellent option.

Connect to the Word

The story of Jesus feeding the crowd with the loaves and fishes (Mark 6:30–44) can help your child understand that it is important to spend time with Jesus and listen to his teaching. Tell the story while showing your child pictures from a children's Bible. Explain that the people were there to be with Jesus. Explain that Jesus loved all the people there and taught them important lessons about how to love God and their neighbor. The people listened to Jesus and paid attention. When the people were hungry, Jesus fed them.

A Closing Meditation: A Reflection on Silence

We need to find God, and he cannot be found in noise and restlessness. God is the friend of silence. See how nature—trees, flowers, grass—grows in silence; see the stars, the moon, and the sun, how they move in silence. We need silence to be able to touch souls.

—Blessed Teresa of Calcutta

We see our daughter Danielle's inability to speak as a type of silence that allows her to connect and commune with God. We have found silence helps us too. Use this passage to reflect on ways you and your family have found God in silence.

2

Cast of Characters

For years Dave had a beard. Sometimes it was close-cropped, and sometimes it was a good deal longer. He had a beard when Danielle was born. When she was a few years old, Dave got tired of the beard and decided to shave. Coming down the stairs clean-shaven, he saw Danielle and said hello. At that moment Danielle burst into tears and moved quickly away from her father. She would not go near Dave. Each time he approached her, she would cry. It was as if she did not recognize her own father. This went on for several hours before she became comfortable with him again and his newly smooth face.

We found out later that it was not uncommon for children with autism to have difficulty recognizing faces and distinguishing among persons. We have heard others tell how a change of hair color or style can produce a lack of recognition of close family members. No one knows for certain why, but sometimes children will use other features to help recognize who people are. We know of a young child with autism who used to go up to any woman with blonde hair because her mother has blonde hair. Most of these children learn to recognize facial features eventually.

In a similar way, children with special needs may have difficulty discriminating between specific objects such as between one school bus and another. As Danielle grew older, someone suggested that if she was taught her bus number, she could find her bus by herself without the assistance of her aide. We are still working on this challenge. Here's another example. Although Danielle can recognize our red van when it is sitting in the driveway, she has considerable difficulty recognizing it in a parking lot where there are other red vans.

The examples we gave in the paragraph above show that children with autism and other disabilities can have a hard time recognizing and discriminating concrete people and objects. Therefore, it makes sense that they may have a difficult time learning about our religious figures, who are more abstract. The following lessons are aimed at helping children with special needs do this.

Lesson 1: Getting to Know Jesus and Mary

Many children with disabilities do not have a clear understanding when their parents and religious educators speak about religious figures. Children are very concrete in their understanding and have trouble with abstract ideas. It is important to make everything you teach as concrete as possible.

For Starters

Teaching a child with special needs about Jesus can be challenging. A good rule is to keep it simple and visual. As part of the *Adaptive First Eucharist Preparation Kit* (Loyola Press, 2012), we developed a picture-based instructional card to emphasize the relational aspects of Jesus to God the Father. It explains that Jesus is God's Son and that Jesus loves us. Danielle knows that we are her mother and father and that we love her. The idea is to use this concrete, nonverbal knowledge as a springboard to the more abstract knowledge of Jesus and God the Father. You can use this piece from our kit or find something similar online or in a picture book. Choose your favorite picture of Jesus. Using your own words, tell your child that Jesus is God's Son. Explain how much God loves Jesus and how much Jesus loves you. This conversation can be combined with role-play, using a plush Jesus figure to make Jesus tangible and meaningful. Plush religious figures can be found in religious supply stores or online. (Loyola Press has a friendly plush figure, Jesus the Teacher, in its *Adaptive Finding God Program*.)

The Fun Begins

Playing dress up is a fun way for children, with special needs or otherwise, to learn about biblical figures. We still remember how our youngest daughter, Shannon, would walk around the house at three years old pretending to be Mary. She wore a blue robe and nightgown with a white bandana while carrying around a baby doll. She informed us that she was Mary and her baby was Jesus. A Mary costume can be as simple as a blue robe and a head covering. Many dress-up items are available at party supply stores or can be adapted from Halloween costumes or from items you have in your closet.

Danielle enjoyed dressing up as an angel, wearing a white dress that was originally a bride costume purchased at a Halloween store. We attached angel wings. You can make a good angel costume using a white T-shirt and sweatpants, with some cardboard and aluminum foil for the wings. A Jesus costume is also easy to make. Use a bathrobe with a rope or sash to tie it closed in the front. A towel can be used as a head covering. A cane can be used as a staff. A pair of sandals completes the costume.

Whatever you do, have fun and be creative!

Religious-themed coloring books are another great way to teach your child about Jesus and Mary. These coloring books often include pictures of scenes from the lives of Jesus and the saints, as well as Bible stories. Remember, even though children with special needs may need support to complete an activity like this, they usually enjoy coloring. Danielle requires hand-over-hand assistance to hold the crayon and color the pictures. Parents can use this activity as an opportunity to connect with their child and have fun at the same time.

Making It Real

One of the nice things about being Catholic is that we have great statues of our religious figures. These can be used to teach children with special needs about Jesus, Mary, Joseph, the Apostles, and the saints. We are fortunate to live near a Cistercian monastery that has a rosary garden. The garden has life-sized statues of Jesus and Mary for each mystery of the rosary. Danielle and Shannon have walked among these statues and in a special way experienced what these events in the life of Jesus and Mary might have been like. You could say that this takes concrete learning to a whole other level! Every Catholic church has statues of Mary and Joseph flanking each side of the altar. So even if you don't live near a rosary garden or a monastery, you can still find suitable representations of religious figures to help teach your child with special needs.

The same principle can be used in other ways. For instance, a fun way to learn about Mary and celebrate her is to participate in a May crowning at your church or school. Better yet, have your own at home!

- Find a statue of Mary, the Mother of God. These come in many sizes and styles. In our home, we have an elegant statue of Mary that is also a vase that holds cut flowers.

- Next, you need flowers. If you have a garden, your children can gather flowers to make into a crown. You can buy flowers at farm stands, florists, and supermarkets. You and your children can even make paper flowers. Roses have been associated with Mary for centuries, but you can use any flower you choose. So pick your favorite flower, enjoy the fragrance, and have fun.

- Have your children stand near the Mary statue and say a prayer. The Hail Mary is our family's favorite.

- If your child is nonverbal but uses an electronic communication device, you can program the prayer into the device. Danielle's device contains several traditional prayers. You can lead the children in any hymn you like, such as "Ave Maria," "Hail Holy Queen," or another one suitable for the occasion.

- The final step is for one of the children to place the crown of flowers on Mary's head or instead to adorn the statue with bouquets.

A Family Story

The time that Shannon spent as a toddler pretending to be Mary prepared her well when she started formal religious education classes. During the May crowning ceremony at her religious education program, our pastor asked the children, "Can anyone tell me about Mary?" A precocious kindergartner raised his hand and said, "Mary is God's wife." The innocence of the boy's response shows how easily young children can be confused about such things. Shannon was happy to provide the correct answer.

Connect to the Word

The *Magnificat* is Mary's beautiful poem of praise and thanksgiving, her joyous response to God's invitation to become the mother of Jesus.

And Mary said:

"My soul magnifies the Lord,
And my spirit rejoices in God my Savior,
For he has looked with favor on the lowliness of
    his servant.
Surely, from now on all generations will call me blessed;
for the Mighty One has done great things for me,
and holy is his name."

—Luke 1:46–49

Read this beautiful passage to your child and explain that Mary is thanking God for sending her Jesus to care for and love. Tell your child how happy you are that God has sent him or her to you.

When you witness your child actively participating and growing in the faith, you may experience something of what Mary felt when singing the *Magnificat*: "The Mighty One has done great things for me." Over the years we have come to see our daughter Danielle's growth in the faith as nothing short of miraculous. We marveled as she learned how to participate in Mass. After receiving Holy

Communion, she quietly kneels with her hands folded in prayer. She extends her hand during the Sign of Peace. We are in awe of what has been accomplished. Not every Sunday is a smooth ride, but we keep coming back, and that is making all the difference.

Lesson 2: God the Father

God is an abstract concept. Jesus as a person lived long ago. We who believe relate to God the Father and to Jesus and feel their continuing presence, but this can be very confusing to children with special needs.

For Starters

Just as we introduced the child to Jesus and Mary by using pictures, we can introduce him or her to God the Father using images too. Find several suitable images of God the Father. Artists through the ages have used their talents to depict God, so you can find great images on the Internet or in art history books. We like the painting by Michelangelo of God creating Adam that adorns the ceiling of the Sistine Chapel in the Vatican. Many children with special needs have their own tablets or devices, which can be useful for searching for and viewing images.

Begin with a matching game. Print out two identical copies of each image. It is helpful to laminate them for durability. Set one copy of each picture in front of your child. Keep the other copies in a pile. Begin by having your child match the first picture in the pile with the corresponding image. Give a clear instruction like "Match the picture!" or "Same to same!" If your child is able to do this accurately without any other prompts, allow him or her to match all the images of God. If needed, provide a hand-over-hand prompt. You can provide reinforcement after each match or after all the matches are completed.

Now let's teach the child to tell the difference between an image of God and a picture of someone else. Choose one of the images of God used before. Next to it place a picture of some other person. Ask the child to point to God. Provide prompts at first and phase them out until he or she can point to God when asked.

The Fun Begins

Children with special needs can have fun learning about God the Father through movies. Depending on the age and cognitive ability of your child, watching movies can be a great way to teach a visually oriented child. While it's hard to find movies about God specifically, you can find movies about Jesus, biblical heroes like Moses, saints like Bernadette, and other important religious figures. These movies can help the child understand and appreciate that sometimes God interacts with people in miraculous ways. Our family loves watching *The Ten Commandments* every Easter. Danielle doesn't watch movies, but many children with special needs do and can even repeat dialogue verbatim.

Making It Real

One way to introduce your child to our rich religious heritage is to visit a cathedral or basilica. Not only are these structures magnificent to look at, but they fill you with awe when you are standing inside them. Visual and experiential learning is important to children with autism and other disabilities. Cathedrals and basilicas are especially good because they present such excellent visual learning opportunities. There are stained-glass windows depicting Jesus, God the Father, the Apostles, martyrs, and saints. Most cathedrals have side chapels with statues, paintings, and frescoes.

Recently, we had the opportunity to visit both St. Patrick's Cathedral in New York City and the Basilica of the National Shrine of the Immaculate Conception in Washington, D.C. We were looking at colleges for our son, and since we were so close to these great churches, we stopped in for a visit. You can spend hours immersed in their majestic beauty.

Not everybody lives in close proximity to these cathedrals, but similar grand structures can be found spread out among our fifty states. Local churches often contain stained glass and other similar features but on a smaller scale and can be visited easily and often.

Connect to the Word

Beloved, let us love one another, because love is from God; everyone who loves is born of God and knows God. Whoever does not love does not know God, for God is love.

—1 John 4:7–8

Explain how much parents love their children. Talk about how God is our Father and loves all of us very much. Let your child know that when we love other people, we love God too.

Lesson 3: The Role of the Priest and Other Religious

Priests and nuns are concrete religious figures whom children meet at church and other places and can be mistaken for our more abstract figures. This is especially so for children with special needs, who may have trouble understanding the distinction between these people and the more abstract figures.

For Starters

Find a picture of a priest. Place this picture next to an image of God. Ask the child, "Which one is God?" Proceed as above until your child is able to point to the image of God, not the picture of the priest. Now ask, "Which one is a priest?" Use hand-over-hand prompts and positive reinforcement as needed until your child can distinguish between God and the priest.

Fortunately, we have priests and nuns in our family. Our children are comfortable being around those in religious life. They are used to sitting across the table at Thanksgiving and Christmas from their great-aunt Kathleen, a Sister of Saint Joseph. Children who are not as familiar with priests and nuns can learn to distinguish them by pointing to pictures with appropriate prompting and reinforcement. For example, you can find plush figures or paper dolls of priests and nuns.

Explain that when a priest celebrates Mass, he is serving God in a special way. Explain that a nun is a woman who also does God's work, but in a different way. Explain that priests and nuns are not married.

The Fun Begins

Some children with special needs like to watch TV and movies. If your child enjoys this, we recommend the movie *The Bells of St. Mary's*. It features Bing Crosby as a priest and Ingrid Bergman as a nun in a Catholic school in the 1940s. Watch the film as a family and explain what's happening in a manner appropriate to your child's level of understanding.

Making It Real

Your local parish is a good place to meet real-life priests and nuns. Our children were fortunate to be exposed to convents at an early age since their great-aunt Kathleen was a Sister of Saint Joseph for more than sixty years. They enjoyed visiting their aunt at the convent and, in later years, at the retirement villa where she resided. In addition, two of our children were taught how to play the piano by Sister Anna Marie. Another sister whom our children have come to know is Sister Clare, who runs the religious education program in our parish. Many local programs are headed up by women religious.

Introduce your child to your parish priest. You can do this after Mass or schedule an appointment. Some children thrive on routine and may expect the same priest to say Mass each time. If this is the case, you can check the Mass schedule to find out which priest is celebrating.

Introduce your child to the nuns at the local convent, parochial school, hospital, or social service agency. Keep in touch on a regular basis. Doing so will allow your child to see the important role of women religious in the Church and in society.

Connect to the Word

"Whoever serves me must follow me, and where I am, there will my servant be also. Whoever serves me, the Father will honor."

—John 12:26

Read the above passage with your child and explain that we are all called to serve God. Discuss ways we can serve God in our lives. Explain that priests and nuns serve God in a special way as leaders in the Church, celebrating Mass, praying, teaching, and helping others.

A Closing Meditation: Mary, the Mother of God

Prayer is powerful beyond limits when we turn to the Immaculata who is queen even of God's heart.

—Saint Maximilian Kolbe

Ave Maria, gratia plena,
Dominus tecum.
Benedicta tu in mulieribus,
et benedictus fructus ventris tui, Iesus.

Hail Mary, full of grace,
the Lord is with thee.
Blessed are you among women
and blessed is the fruit
of thy womb, Jesus.

Find a quiet place to meditate on Saint Maximilian Kolbe's statement above. Think about times in your life when you have turned to Mary for intercession and guidance. Consider how you might feel if you had never learned about Mary nor been taught to turn to her. Imagine Mary teaching young Jesus about God the Father and the Old Testament patriarchs and prophets. Now visualize yourself teaching your child with the love and enthusiasm that Mary must have shown.

3

First Holy Communion

Often people are concerned or even alarmed that a child with cognitive impairment might be allowed to receive the precious Body and Blood of Jesus without an adequate understanding of what it means. Rose, an acquaintance, certainly was concerned, and she told us so. She meant well when she asked us if Danielle truly understood that the host becomes the Body and Blood of Jesus during Holy Communion. "Surely she doesn't need the sacrament," Rose suggested. After all, wasn't she an angel already in the eyes of God?

We considered the issue. In those days, we were not even sure ourselves whether five-year-old Danielle would ever be able to receive the sacrament. Autism can be very difficult for both child and family especially at this age. It was a time of stress and uncertainty and void of clear direction. We were still coming to grips with the fact that our little girl had such a serious disability. Naturally when faced with uncertainty it is comforting to seek the guidance and advice of those whose opinion you value. In this case, however, the advice was unsolicited and unwelcome. How dare she? During the consecration the priest holds up the host and repeats the words of Jesus: "Take this ALL of you and eat." The word "all" resonated in our minds. We knew that our daughter Danielle was part of that "ALL."

While there was perhaps some merit to Rose's concern, we knew that you didn't need a theologian's grasp of the concept of transubstantiation to receive the sacrament. "Well, does anyone really understand?" we responded. "It is, after all, a mystery!" In our hearts we knew that Danielle could learn to do it. We knew she could see Jesus in the sacrament if she was given the opportunity and proper supports. Already we had seen her make considerable progress in other areas, such as learning to communicate with pictures. She was even able to tolerate wearing eyeglasses. We were sure she could do it, but how?

What we didn't know but soon found out is that the U.S. bishops have published a set of guidelines for people with disabilities to receive their sacraments. They recognized what we had intuitively thought. You don't have to be Thomas Aquinas. The main criterion is that the child can distinguish the Body of Christ from ordinary food. The child doesn't even have to identify it with Jesus, only to know that it is special and deserves reverence. In other words, the child must receive the host in a reverent way. The bishops also note that the child must have the use of reason, but they very clearly state that "Cases of doubt should be resolved in favor of the right of the baptized person to receive the sacrament."

We understood the bishops' requirements were minimal, and we hoped that Danielle could learn not only to differentiate the host from ordinary food but also associate the host with Jesus. We worked out a plan with the approval of her catechist to use a specialized approach and specialized learning materials. Our family made a series of materials ourselves using pictures, which we laminated. The homemade materials later became the basis for the *Adaptive First Eucharist Preparation Kit* (Loyola Press, 2012). This was still a long way off though. We muddled through, but as we had hoped, Danielle was able to demonstrate to our parish catechist that she had satisfied the requirements and even gone beyond them to associate the host with Jesus.

Danielle's First Holy Communion was an experience we would never forget. On a beautiful August night in 2006, Danielle was able to receive her First Holy Communion and the Sacrament of Reconciliation. We both remember being terribly nervous. Would she reverently take the host? Would this be her first and last Communion? Again, autism has been one of our greatest challenges in life and the source of some of our greatest blessings. Clearly, Danielle making her First Holy Communion that summer night was one such blessing. Danielle reverently received Communion that night and continues to do so. And as it does for many of us, her reverence and understanding of the sacrament continue to deepen.

Lesson 1: Communion Is Not the Same as Food

In order to receive Holy Communion, children with disabilities must be able to distinguish the host from ordinary food.

For Starters

You can use unconsecrated hosts to introduce your child to the Sacrament of Holy Communion. These hosts can be obtained from your parish. Ask the Director of Religious Education or the catechist you are working with to bring these to your home. These are unconsecrated hosts that will be used for teaching purposes only. These visits from the DRE or catechist will provide an additional opportunity to ensure that all necessary content is being taught and mastered.

- You or the catechist can begin by showing the unconsecrated host to your child and allowing him or her to hold it and feel its shape and size, its texture and light weight.

- Next, place a preferred food item—in Danielle's case, a small cracker—a few inches from the unconsecrated host.

- Explain to your child that both items can be eaten but that the host is very special. It is not ordinary food. It becomes Jesus during Mass.

- Invite your child to touch the host. Provide a hand-over-hand prompt if needed. Offer verbal praise to reinforce the correct choice.

- Ask your child to touch the food item. You can say something like, "Touch the food." Provide a hand-over-hand prompt as needed. To reinforce that this is indeed food, allow the child to eat the food item.

- Alternate asking the child to touch the host and asking the child to touch the food. Use prompts as needed to ensure continued success. Reinforce as above. Do multiple trials of each, and fade out prompts and reinforcers as able.

The Fun Begins

The task of teaching your child to distinguish the host from ordinary food does not have to be complicated. You can easily make a matching game to teach that the host belongs with Jesus and not food. All you need are three pictures: a host, Jesus, and food. These pictures can be laminated for durability. The idea is for the child to successfully place the picture of the host next to the picture of Jesus and not next to the picture of food. A puzzle version of this activity is available as part of the *Adaptive First Eucharist Preparation Kit* (Loyola Press, 2012).

- Place the picture of Jesus on the left side of your workspace and the picture of food on the right side.

- Give the picture of the host to your child and say, "Does communion go with Jesus or with food?"

- Use a hand-over-hand prompt to place the picture of the host below the picture of Jesus. Reinforce with a preferred item or activity, such as verbal praise, deep pressure, or a high five. Repeat this activity several times.

- Then rearrange the pictures so that they are reversed; that is, place the picture of food on the left and the picture of Jesus on the right.

- Continue as above so that the child can consistently place the picture of the host below the picture of Jesus. Phase out the prompts and reinforcers until your child can do this successfully without help.

Since you are working on this regularly with the parish catechist, the catechist can use the opportunity to emphasize any required content. As mentioned above, she can also determine when your child has successfully satisfied all requirements and is properly prepared to receive the sacrament.

Making It Real

Visit your church at a quiet time when Mass is not being celebrated. Sit in your preferred pew. Point out the altar and explain that this is where the priest changes the host into Jesus. Explain that it will still look, feel, and taste like the host did before. Now point out the tabernacle. Explain that this is where hosts are kept.

Practice exiting the pew into the aisle. Walk up in the manner that you would to receive communion. Return to the pew. Practice kneeling, blessing yourself, and saying a brief prayer. Work up to attending the least crowded Mass of the weekend. Eventually, you will want to attend your preferred Mass. Remember to offer breaks when you feel your child needs them.

Connect to the Word

Then he took a loaf of bread, and when he had given thanks, he broke it and gave it to them, saying, "This is my body, which is given for you. Do this in remembrance of me." And he did the same with the cup after supper, saying, "This cup that is poured out for you is the new covenant in my blood."

—Luke 22:19–20

Find this passage about the institution of the Eucharist at the Last Supper in your Children's Bible. Read the passage or tell the story in your own words. Emphasize that we receive communion at church to remember Jesus and be with him.

Download a picture of Leonardo da Vinci's painting *The Last Supper*. Point out Jesus and the Apostles. Discuss the story in a way your child can understand.

Lesson 2: Reverent Reception of Holy Communion

Receiving the host reverently takes practice. Children with disabilities may not understand what reverence means. Reverent behavior, however, can be taught with careful instruction, including reinforcement for appropriate behaviors and not reinforcing the wrong behaviors. It is well worth the effort and is essential in order to receive the Sacrament of Holy Eucharist.

For Starters

It is only natural to be concerned about whether your child will be able to ingest the host in a reverent manner. It was certainly a big fear for us. We worried that Danielle would not like the taste and might spit the host out. Like many other children with disabilities, Danielle has sensitivities to various food textures and tastes, especially unfamiliar ones, so practice using unconsecrated hosts was essential.

Offer your child an unconsecrated host. If your child consumes it fully without any problems, offer verbal praise. If not, continue practicing until the host is tolerated. If your child has any difficulty consuming the host, do the following:

- Place a small piece of the unconsecrated host on a plate along with a small bite of your child's favorite snack.
- Offer the piece of the host first. Quickly follow this with the snack. Vary the size of each piece, either smaller or larger, until your child can tolerate the host.
- Continue multiple trials. Gradually increase the size of the host and decrease the size of the food item until your child can consume the host without the other food item.

Don't be too concerned if your child cannot tolerate an entire host. You can walk with your child in the communion line and signal for the priest or Eucharistic minister that a small piece of host is needed.

Danielle received a small piece of the host for years. We are happy to report that she was eventually able to receive a full host, and she has always received reverently.

The Fun Begins

There is a lot to learn when preparing for First Holy Communion, including reverent behavior in the Communion line, proper hand placement when receiving, and giving some form of consent to the priest or Eucharistic minister. Practicing each of these elements ahead of time is key. If children know what is being asked and expected of them, they will rise to the occasion.

Invite friends and siblings to help your child practice proper reverence in receiving Communion by doing the following:

- Once again, visit your church at a time when Mass is not in session. Have everyone start in the pew as if it is time to go up for Communion. Many children with special needs will need a parent or caretaker to escort them in the Communion line. You might arrange to have a sibling or two in front of and behind your child with special needs.

- In an orderly fashion have the first child exit the pew, followed by the others to form a communion line. Make sure you are standing behind your child. You may choose to guide your child by placing your hands on the child's shoulders if this is tolerated.

- Ask the DRE or catechist to act out the part of the Eucharistic minister. As the line moves forward, you can provide appropriate physical prompts as needed to maintain an orderly procession.

- As you approach the "Eucharistic minister," use a hand-over-hand prompt to position your child's hands properly: palms up with one hand on top of the other.

- The "Eucharistic minister" says, "The Body of Christ." Your child makes whatever response he or she can: vocal approximation of "Amen," reverential silence, head nod, or something similar. The "Eucharistic minister" gives the child the unconsecrated host to consume.

- Return in an orderly fashion to the pew to kneel with hands folded in prayer if able.

Practice this as many times as needed. You may try teaching the more complicated portions of the sequence such as hand placement and consent as individual components before putting it all together. Gradually fade out the prompts and supports as much as you can. However, know that some level of support is permissible during Mass. We still escort Danielle in line and help with proper hand placement for receipt, as the complex mechanics of this continue to be confusing to her. Your DRE can inform the parish priest and Eucharistic ministers about the supports your child needs.

Making It Real

As you have been working closely with your local parish DRE to prepare your child for the sacraments, your DRE can arrange an opportunity for you to meet with the pastor and Eucharistic ministers. This meeting will give you an opportunity to brief them on anything you think they will need to know to ensure a successful First Communion, including details about the types of supports that will be needed. For instance, you can explain that you will be assisting your child in the communion line or that you will signal for a small piece of the host rather than an entire host. Explain details about your child's communication abilities and style. Things work out best when everyone knows what to expect.

Connect to the Word

One thing I asked of the LORD,
    that will I seek after:
to live in the house of the LORD
    all the days of my life,
to behold the beauty of the LORD,
    and to inquire in his temple.

—Psalm 27:4

Read this psalm aloud to your children and explain that all churches are God's house, where we behave in a special way.

Drive to two or three nearby churches. Emphasize that Jesus is present in the Bread and Wine, and that we should be on our best behavior whenever we are in a church.

Lesson 3: Practical Considerations

Preparing for and receiving First Holy Communion is an exciting time and one you will want to celebrate with your child and family. Practical consideration should be given to what clothing and shoes your child will wear, the physical layout of the church, and whether or not your child should receive in a group setting or something more private.

For Starters

Most likely you will want your child to wear a special outfit, though this is not mandatory. Certain things need to be taken into consideration, including how comfortable your child will be in a communion suit and tie, or dress and veil. Some children may have problems with clothing tags, certain fabrics, and other aspects of the wardrobe. It's best to practice wearing these clothes in advance of the big day, even if it's just around the house. Children may have gait issues and it might be a good idea to practice walking in dressy shoes or other attire.

The Fun Begins

You may wish to help your child send a personalized invitation to attend the First Communion service and a personalized thank-you note afterward. One way we added a special touch to our daughter's First Communion was to send our family and friends an invitation to the event in the way Danielle communicates using picture icons. The invitation was easy to make and especially meaningful to Danielle.

You can do something similar.

Use Boardmaker or a related software product to make picture icons. Decide what you wish to say. If your child is computer savvy, he or she can design and print the invitation. Or if you prefer, help your child cut out the icons and paste them onto a piece of background paper. Address the invitations and help your child use a stamp to sign them.

Making It Real

Deciding whether your child should receive First Communion in a group setting with the entire religious education class or during an ordinary Mass is important. Some children do well following and remembering directions, or they can follow along with their peers. Some children, however, may do better in the more familiar setting of an ordinary Mass. There is less noise and less distraction. The child is in the pew with parents who can monitor behavior and provide prompts and reassurance as needed. The proximity to parents is especially important if your child needs you to escort him or her in the communion line, assist with hand placement when receiving, or signal for a smaller piece of the host. Danielle received her First Communion at an ordinary Mass for many of these reasons. Parents should weigh the pros and cons of each option for their child and consult with their child's catechist or the parish Director of Religious Education when making their decision.

Connect to the Word

"Therefore I tell you, do not worry about your life, what you will eat or what you will drink, or about your body, what you will wear. Is not life more than food, and the body more than clothing? Look at the birds of the air; they neither sow nor reap nor gather into barns, and yet your heavenly Father feeds them. Are you not of more value than they? And can any of you by worrying add a single hour to your span of life? And why do you worry about clothing? Consider the lilies of the field, how they grow; they neither toil nor spin, yet I tell you, even Solomon in all his glory was not clothed like one of these. But if God so clothes the grass of the field, which is alive today and tomorrow is thrown into the oven, will he not more clothe you . . .?"

—Matthew 6:25–30

Sometimes worry can consume us and stop us from taking important steps in our lives and the lives of our children. When confronted with the uncertainties of their children's behavior, parents of children with special needs may feel overwhelmed. At such times we can remember the words of Jesus and trust that God will provide what we need. So take a few deep breaths, and look at the birds and the flowers and the grass. Do what needs to be done, and proceed without fear or worry.

A Closing Meditation: God Knows Us

Christ in the tabernacle sees and knows us far more clearly than we see and know ourselves. The knowledge of us that exists within the sacramental Christ whom we receive in Communion is a knowledge He has already gained from the depths of our own being.

—Thomas Merton

4

Reconciliation

Our son Colin was about ten years old when he complained to us that "Danielle can do anything she wants without any consequences." Poor Colin had just left a trail of Cheerios on the floor and he was now being handed a broom and dust pan to clean it up. "You never make Danielle clean up her messes," he said. "But the rest of us have to fix it and say we're sorry. It's not fair."

This brief exchange with Colin made us recognize that it was important for our other children to see that Danielle was not exempt from receiving appropriate consequences. We sensed that Danielle was capable of knowing at least on some level when she had done something wrong and that she could, in much the same way as her siblings, take at least some action to fix the problem, even if this meant that she needed our help to do it properly. So the next time we found a trail of Cheerios leading to Danielle, we gave her the dust pan and helped her with the cleanup. Danielle seemed happy to help. Her brothers and sister looked on approvingly.

Coincidentally, this conversation occurred around the time Danielle was preparing for her First Communion. We had been on the fence with whether or not she would need to receive the Sacrament of Reconciliation prior to Communion. Our pastor and others had told us it would not be necessary since Danielle could receive a dispensation. Yet, with the "Cheerios incident" still fresh in our minds, we knew we wanted her to receive the Sacrament of Reconciliation anyway. We knew that there would be value in such a powerful and immediate sign of God's love and forgiveness.

Although she could not receive Reconciliation in the traditional way due to her lack of language, she was able to use augmentative communication. Her primary method of communication in those days was through the Picture Exchange Communication System (PECS). Danielle carried with her a small binder with laminated picture icons attached by Velcro. She would select a picture and hand it to the person with whom she was communicating. She could exchange a card showing the "I'm Sorry" icon with the priest to make her confession in a simple but poignant exchange.

We made arrangements with our pastor for Danielle to make both sacraments on the same day. We arrived with Danielle before Mass and entered the Reconciliation room where Father sat. Danielle made the Sign of the Cross and then picked up the "I'm Sorry" icon. She reached across the table and gave it to the priest. He accepted it and granted her absolution.

Danielle received enormous graces that day. Graces that she might have missed had it not been for some spilled Cheerios. God provides his guidance and support in our lives in the most unpredictable ways, if we are open to God's love and present to those around us.

Lesson 1: Right Versus Wrong

Knowing right from wrong can be difficult at times for all of us. Children with special needs can have a particularly difficult time of it since their cognitive deficits may interfere with their ability to judge the full consequences of their actions.

For Starters

It is important to look for naturally occurring examples of right and wrong actions. Any given day presents opportunities to teach your child how to distinguish good choices from bad choices and to act accordingly. Parents will find occasions in the natural environment to teach good manners, proper care of one's personal items, and how to get along with siblings, friends, parents, and teachers. We look for opportunities to shape our children's behavior in a positive direction by modeling and reinforcing correct choices. We do this for all of our children, not just Danielle. Nearly all children will respond to positive reinforcement. We continue to provide verbal praise to our children with sentences that sound like the following examples:

"I like the way you made your bed."
"Thank you for helping me clean up your toys."
"You were so nice to your sister today. I know that meant a lot to her."

The Fun Begins

As we have seen above, natural environment training can be a great way to teach your child with special needs about making good choices. Another great way to teach and reinforce making good choices and avoiding bad choices would be a simple activity called Good Choice/Bad Choice Cards. You can make these cards yourself or use the set that comes in the *Adaptive Reconciliation Kit* (Loyola Press, 2012).

Each card shows a picture of a child engaged in either a good behavior or bad behavior. These cards come in pairs, such as Sharing/Not Sharing, In Control/Out of Control, or Respectful/Disrespectful.

These cards can be used in different ways. One way is to have your child learn to sort the cards into good choices and bad choices.

- Begin with three or four pairs of cards face down on the table.
- Designate one side of the work space for good choices and one side for bad choices.
- Turn over the first pair of cards and explain each to your child in an appropriate way that your child can understand.
- Ask your child, "Is this a good choice or a bad choice?"
- Provide a hand-over-hand prompt to place each card in the appropriate column to indicate the correct response.
- Remember to reinforce each correct response with something your child likes.

Making It Real

Build on the ability to distinguish good and bad choices by teaching your child to say he is sorry when he does something wrong. Children with special needs, like all children, need to learn to acknowledge their bad choices by saying they are sorry. This is very important when a child takes something that belongs to another child, bumps into someone else, damages property, or acts in an unkind way.

Many children with special needs have language deficits and may have difficulty verbally communicating to others that they are sorry. Fortunately there are other ways to communicate.

Vocal Approximation Some children with limited language skills can still make vocal sounds that approximate words and phrases. Any attempt, even if only partially recognizable, should count here.

Picture Icons Many children use picture icons to communicate. This can take the form of a physical Picture Exchange Communication System (PECS) icon or an electronic augmentative communication system. PECS was developed in 1985 by Lori Frost and Andy Bondy. These communication systems are widely used by children with communication issues. Danielle uses pictures for most of her communication needs.

Sign Language Children with disabilities often communicate using American Sign Language (ASL) or other sign language systems.

Some children use a combination of these methods. Regardless of which method is chosen you can teach your child some way to say, "I'm sorry." Be alert to naturally occurring opportunities for your child to tell someone "I'm sorry," using his or her preferred method of communication. You will likely need to point out to your child when an apology is in order and why. Then provide an appropriate prompt to gain the attention of the other party. A good way to do this is to visually model it and see if he or she can imitate you. Danielle sometimes takes food from her siblings at mealtime. We explain that the food doesn't belong to her. Then we model the sign for "I'm sorry." Danielle will imitate the sign and make a verbal approximation. Her siblings will respond, "That's okay, Danielle." If needed, you can use a hand-over-hand prompt to exchange an "I'm sorry" PECS icon, or use an electronic device. If your child is more comfortable with sign language, he or she can sign "I'm sorry." As always, reinforce success. You might try verbal praise, such as "I'm so proud of you when you say you are sorry!" At some point, your child may initiate "I'm sorry" with less reliance on prompts or perhaps even independently.

Connect to the Word

"Pray then in this way:

Our Father in heaven,
hallowed be your name.
Your kingdom come.
Your will be done,
on earth as it is in heaven.
Give us today our daily bread.
And forgive us our debts,
as we also have forgiven our debtors.
And do not bring us to the time of trial,
but rescue us from the evil one."

—Matthew 6:9–13

Although the language of this passage may be challenging for children to understand, parents can paraphrase and simplify the words. Loyola Press publishes a Lord's Prayer flip book with picture icons on each page to help explain the meaning of the prayer. Explain to your child how important it is to God that we not only ask forgiveness when we have injured someone else, but also we must forgive others when they have caused us harm.

Lesson 2: First Reconciliation

The actual mechanics of the Sacrament of Reconciliation can be a challenge. Children with special needs may require more support to perform the actions of examination of conscience, confession, and act of contrition due to their language barriers and supervision level.

For Starters

Before receiving the Sacrament of Reconciliation your child should perform an examination of conscience. However, the form this takes will vary depending on the child's cognitive level. Some children, especially those who function in higher cognitive ranges, will be very much aware of specific sins they have committed. Traditionally, an examination of conscience might involve going through the Ten Commandments and asking yourself questions about your behavior relative to each commandment. A child with Asperger syndrome or high functioning autism could probably do this. You can find examples of such formal examinations of conscience on the Internet.

Other children may not have this ability but will be able to express a general awareness of wrongdoing. Many children with special needs will need a highly modified version of the examination of conscience. Pictures can make it easier to understand. The *Adaptive Reconciliation Kit* (Loyola Press, 2013) contains a useful examination of conscience card with illustrated questions, such as the following:

Do I love God first?
Do I love my family?
Do I love my neighbor?
Do I listen to my parents?
Do I share?
Do I say nice things?

The beauty of this version lies in its simplicity and flexibility. However, many children may need you to pose these questions in a slightly different way. Try asking your child, "What would I like to do better?" The idea is for them to respond by pointing to a picture that shows what they want to do better. One child might choose an icon that shows "Listening to my parents." Another might choose "Praying more." Still another might show that they wish to "Help people." Some children might be able to use the examination of conscience card in the Reconciliation room the way they would use an augmentative device to communicate to the priest. Most will use it beforehand to prepare themselves before making their confession. And some children will not be able to use this examination of conscience because it is too complex given their cognitive level. Danielle was unable to use it, but many children in the small group program she attended are able to use it as described above.

The Fun Begins

Social stories are an effective tool for teaching children with autism and other disabilities how to manage new situations. A social story can introduce your child to the process of Reconciliation before he or she actually enters the confessional or Reconciliation room. The key to a good social story is that the new event is presented along with any possible variations that might be encountered. For example, the child might confess to different priests, and may choose to confess face to face versus behind a screen, or there may be a long wait. Anticipating these scenarios and potential variations can help to alleviate anxiety and frustration. Preparing the child ahead of time can help things go more smoothly.

You can write your own social story targeted to the specific needs of your child. Here are some guidelines:

- Place your child directly in the story as a character and refer to him or her by name.

- Limit each page to one line of text. You can include a picture icon to illustrate the main point of each page.

- Present the various parts of the sacrament in simple words the child can understand.

- Introduce any potential variations, letting the child know that sometimes different things can happen and that this is okay.

- Read the story to your child as many times as you like. Each time that you do it will let your child know what to expect, and they will feel more comfortable with the process.

If you would rather use a published social story instead, you can find a good one in the *Adaptive Reconciliation Kit*.

Prepare your child to allow him or her to receive the sacrament independently, if possible. To achieve this, children can benefit from repeatedly practicing the steps of the sacrament. Ask your child's catechist to review and practice the steps to the receiving the Sacrament of Reconciliation. Arrange for your child and pastor to establish familiarity with each other and with your child's communication style and abilities, whether it is spoken, written, or through an electronic device. If your child is unable to receive the sacrament independently, he or she can be accompanied by an interpreter. The catechist, trusted adult, or, if necessary, parent accompanying the child as an interpreter should be educated so as to have an understanding of the Seal of the Confessional. Alternatively, you may wish to attend a parish communal Reconciliation service.

Making It Real

The Sacrament of Reconciliation seems complex, but according to the USCCB *Guidelines for the Celebration of the Sacraments with Persons with Disabilities* (no. 23):

> As long as the individual is capable of having a sense of contrition for having committed sin, even if he or she cannot describe the

sin precisely in words, the person may receive sacramental absolution. . . . In the case of individuals with poor communication skills, sorrow for sin is to be accepted even if this repentance is expressed through some gesture rather than verbally.

Again, there is a wide range of abilities among children with special needs. Some will be able to perform the sacrament independently, and some will require added supports. Modifications could include the following:

Interpreter Your child may initially need an interpreter in the confessional or Reconciliation room. It is our hope and prayer that every parish will be able to provide the support of an intrepreter. The interpreter will help him or her sequence the steps of the sacrament, and communicate with the priest when needed. The interpreter may provide prompts as needed and help the child in other ways. Whether the interpreter is a catechist or other adult known and trusted by the child, his or her assistance should be phased out as soon as possible. It was necessary for us to accompany Danielle when she received Reconciliation.

Augmentative Communication In the previous lesson we discussed different ways a child with communication issues might confess his or her sins to the priest and express contrition. If a child is able, he might show a Bad Choice card to the priest, or even point to the appropriate icons on the Examination of Conscience card. These options will be appropriate for certain children but may be beyond the ability of others. If so, then the child can exchange an "I'm sorry" card, sign "I'm sorry," or push the "I'm sorry" button on an electronic device.

Penance Children who can recite formal prayers can pray a traditional penance. Others might pray a prayer you stored on the augmentative communication device. Danielle has several prayers available on her speech machine. Some children may pray by pressing hands together in the prayer position or making the Sign of the Cross. You can visually model this or prompt in necessary ways.

If the above modifications are not suitable given the needs of your child, an alternative option is to participate in a communal penitential service. Talk with your catechist, DRE, and pastor about this option.

Connect to the Word

If we confess our sins, he who is faithful and just will forgive us our sins and cleanse us from all unrighteousness.

—1 John 1:9

Let your child know when we confess our sins and are forgiven, we feel peaceful. And assure them that they can make good choices and avoid bad ones. Emphasize that God loves us and forgives us when we do wrong.

A Closing Meditation: Trust in Him Alone

I believe that God helps those who set out to do great things for His sake and never fails those who trust in Him alone.

—Saint Teresa of Ávila

As humans we will all make mistakes in our lives. It is not easy raising children with special needs. We may find it hard to make good choices and avoid bad choices ourselves. We need to remember that even when we sin, God is there to help us and strengthen us. God invites us to receive the Sacrament of Reconciliation too. God gives us the grace to rise above our own failings and limitations. We simply need to trust the power of God's grace and allow him to raise us up to be strong and morally fit. In this way we can be good role models for our children and there for them when they need us.

5

Confirmation

A newly ordained bishop had just arrived in our diocese, and we were honored that ours was his very first Confirmation. The ceremony began like any other with a procession of adolescents making their way from the entrance of the church. It was beautiful to see our friend Nicholas in his wheelchair and Danielle next to him, each leading the procession. Afterward, the bishop told the Confirmation coordinator, "Nicholas and Danielle were filled with the Holy Spirit long before that day." Of course we always knew this in our hearts, but it was nice to hear it validated by the bishop.

Before the procession we were nervous that Danielle would not do well in a group Confirmation. When she received her First Communion, she was the only child making the sacrament. Now at Confirmation, there would be a crowd of children, extra noise, and a longer-than-usual liturgy. This unfamiliar event could pose problems for Danielle who, like many children with special needs, prefers familiar routines. But when the bishop traced her forehead with Chrism and anointed her using the name Grace, we knew we could relax as we felt God's presence and love on that special day.

Since Danielle is nonverbal and unable to tell us her choice of a Confirmation name, the decision fell to us. For years we had been making decisions and advocating for her to the best of our ability, trying to judge what was best for her and what she would like. Trying to anticipate the wishes and desires of another person is a lot of responsibility, even for seemingly small decisions. For a child, though, choosing a Confirmation name is a big decision. Danielle's older brothers had made their choices independently. Even if we had tried, we couldn't have steered Colin away from Saint Christopher, the patron saint of basketball, or influenced Brendan to reject the brainy Saint Thomas Aquinas. These names and the saints who inspired them were meaningful in the context of both our sons' lives. Help your child select a meaningful saint's name.

At her Baptism we had selected Mary to be Danielle's middle name in honor of her grandmother who had passed away shortly before. For Confirmation, we decided to expand on this. The name Mary brings to mind the beautiful prayer we all know so well: "Hail Mary, full of grace, the Lord is with you." Like other parents raising children with special needs, we knew the need for grace all too well. We decided that her Confirmation name would be Grace.

Another reason we chose the name was to honor our friend Grace, whom we met through the Special Disciples Program at our parish. This was the religious education program for children with special needs. Not only did Grace prepare Danielle for the sacraments, but she also spent countless hours giving of her time and developing her ministry to enable many other children to take part in the sacramental life of the Church. Grace recognized when children needed one-on-one instruction and when small groups would suffice. In many ways, Grace was the catalyst for Danielle's religious development. So when it came time to pick a Confirmation sponsor for Danielle, we asked Grace.

After the ceremony, we breathed a sigh of relief. Again, everything went as planned. Danielle behaved appropriately. She received the Holy Spirit. God had called her and each of her classmates in a very special way and by a very special name. God's grace filled all our hearts.

Lesson 1: Baptismal Promises

"All baptized, unconfirmed Catholics who possess the use of reason may receive the sacrament of confirmation if they are suitably instructed, properly disposed and able to renew their baptismal promises (Canon 889). Persons who because of developmental or mental disabilities may never attain the use of reason are to be encouraged either directly or, if necessary, through their parents or guardian, to receive the sacrament of confirmation at the appropriate time."

—*Guidelines for the Celebration of the Sacraments with Persons with Disabilities,* no. 16

For Starters

The Sacrament of Confirmation has become an important Catholic rite of passage from childhood into adulthood. It is a time for shedding childhood reliance on our parents and taking on more responsibility in our own spiritual lives. At Baptism, our parents and godparents made promises on our behalf. At Confirmation, we renew these promises ourselves. Like the rest of us, children with special needs have come a long way. They are much more capable and self-reliant. They need less support and have learned to do many things themselves. Increased maturity brings increased responsibility, including at least to some degree participating in a renewal of baptismal promises.

Begin by asking, "What is a promise?" Explain to your child that when you promise to do something, you try your best to do it. For some children, the definition of a promise may be too abstract. You will have to modify or adjust it to meet their level of understanding. You can make the concept as simple and concrete as you need it to be. You want to communicate that keeping the promise is necessary because people are depending on you. You might phrase promises like this:

"You promised to walk the dog."
"You promised to do the dishes."
"You promised to make your bed."
"You promised to take out the garbage."

You can move from here to asking the child, "What would happen if you didn't walk the dog?" You could explain that the dog is counting on getting some exercise and fresh air, and that when you promise something it is important to follow through. Our daughter Shannon promised our neighbors that she would take care of their dogs while they were on vacation, which required that she visit the dogs four times a day to feed them and give them outdoor exercise. Although this was a lot of work, Shannon kept her promise. The dogs were very excited when Shannon came to see them. They were counting on her, and she did a great job. This helped Shannon understand on a deeper level the importance of keeping promises.

Remind your child that he or she was a baby once. Show the child pictures of his or her Baptism and point out the godparents. Explain how they promised that the child would love God and do good things.

Tell your child that he or she will have another special day called Confirmation when he or she will remember these promises, say yes to them, and promise to keep them himself or herself. Of course, the parish catechist will teach the content and meaning of the baptismal promises that are to be renewed at confirmation, but it would be helpful for you as the parent to put this in a personal context so your child can better understand and relate to Confirmation as an unfolding of his or her Baptism.

The Fun Begins

Confirmation is the sacramental affirmation of the Holy Spirit in our lives. As parents supporting the work of the parish catechist, our job is to make this idea concrete so that our child can comprehend it.

The Sign of the Cross is one of the best ways to remind your child about the Holy Spirit because it invokes the whole Trinity. Remind your child that when we pray the Sign of the Cross, we bless ourselves "In the name of the Father, and of the Son, and of the Holy Spirit. Amen." For years we had to provide hand-over-hand assistance for Danielle to successfully complete this difficult sequence. Fortunately, she had been introduced to the Sign of the Cross because we had worked with her special-needs catechist. Danielle spent many sessions at home learning to cross herself when she was preparing for the Sacrament of the Eucharist. Even after making her First Communion, she needed assistance and prompts. Whenever the opportunity presented itself, we would help Danielle make the Sign of the Cross at the appropriate time—during the liturgy, blessing herself with holy water, saying grace each night at dinner, or at bedtime prayers. You can imagine how overjoyed we were when one day during Mass we noticed Danielle placing her hand on her forehead and performing all the steps of the Sign of the Cross without assistance or prompting. Now Danielle has learned to respond appropriately when anyone begins the prayer.

Other ways to help your child understand and appreciate the importance of the Holy Spirit include the following:

- Light a candle and use its flame to light two other candles. Explain that just as the three candles come from the same flame, the Father, Son, and Holy Spirit are one God.

- Explain that the Holy Spirit is the active presence of God in our lives. It is like the wind, invisible but powerful. To illustrate this, show your child how a fan can blow papers across the room. Better yet, fly a kite on a windy day or play with a pinwheel to show the invisible power of wind. Tell your child that this Spirit will fill his or her heart and help him or her to make good choices.

Making It Real

Christian service is an important part of preparation for the Sacrament of Confirmation. As we mature in the faith, we realize that God calls us to help others. Children with special needs can learn to help others and should be included as much as possible in Christian service activities. We explore service more fully in Chapter 7, but Confirmation provides an excellent opportunity to lay the foundations for this important mark of discipleship.

Finding service opportunities for children with special needs, who are more often the recipients of other people's kindness and good deeds, might at times seem easier said than done. However, opportunities for our children to make a meaningful difference in the lives of others certainly exist. You never know when such opportunities will arise, but you have to make a conscious effort to respond to these opportunities when they do.

One such time was when Danielle was in line with us at the supermarket in the express lane. A woman came up behind us in a motorized shopping cart with a basket full of groceries and said, "Excuse me, but I need your teenager to help me unload my shopping cart onto the checkout belt." We did a double take since we are not used to such requests being made to Danielle. Most people can sense that she might not be the best choice to give assistance. Unfortunately, we are more accustomed to stares and glances or to people nervously looking away. This woman did not notice anything different or unusual about Danielle. All she knew was that she was tired from shopping and needed someone to help her. So after a brief pause we said, "Of course she can help, and we will too." Danielle was delighted to help out and had a huge smile on her face as she listened to our verbal prompts and successfully unloaded the woman's cart. Clearly, the Gifts of the Holy Spirit to know God's will and to do God's will were on display. We were afforded wisdom, courage, and right judgment to let her try.

Danielle was given understanding, knowledge, and reverence. All present were filled with wonder and awe. We learned that when there is an opportunity to assist someone in some way, trust the Holy Spirit and give it a shot.

Connect to the Word

"But you will receive power when the Holy Spirit has come upon you; and you will be my witnesses."

—Acts of the Apostles 1:8

Explain that after Jesus went back to Heaven, he sent the Holy Spirit so that we would become filled with the power of God's love and do good in the world. Explain that we receive this power at Confirmation when we receive the Gifts of the Holy Spirit.

Lesson 2: Choosing a Name and a Sponsor

There are several aspects of the Sacrament of Confirmation that can be challenging for children with autism and other disabilities. Choosing a Confirmation name, selecting a sponsor, and tolerating being anointed with Chrism by the bishop or other celebrant may be difficult for a child with special needs.

For Starters

When our son Brendan was about five years old, he discovered that his middle name, David, was the same as his father's first name. This so delighted him that he would go out of his way to let everyone, especially his brother Colin, know that his name was really Brendan David. Colin was three years old and hadn't quite figured out this middle name business. He just knew that it must be something pretty good since his brother was so happy about it. So whenever Brendan said, "My name is Brendan David," Colin answered, "And my name is Colin David." It didn't matter that we all told him his middle name was actually John, after his grandfather; he was insistent. When Brendan would lord it over him and say, "Your name is not Colin David; it's Colin John," a tearful Colin would appeal to his mother to resolve the issue. Sleep deprived after recently giving birth to Danielle and dealing with the two young boys, she told him, "We will just change it to Colin David then!" This was simply too much for Brendan, who was adamant that you could not just change your name. It wasn't allowed!

We share this story because one characteristic of autism is cognitive rigidity and extreme reliance on rules. Of course there is a wide spectrum of behavior and this may not be a problem for all children with autism, but some children might react negatively to the thought of having their name changed, modified, or otherwise tinkered with.

"What do you mean I'm going to get a new name at Confirmation? I like the one I have." As a parent of a child with special needs, you can almost feel the anxiety starting to build. It's important to introduce this to your child in a way that minimizes such problems.

Find a saint to whom your child can relate. It is always helpful if that saint embodies something that appeals to your child or who has a similar interest or characteristic. For instance, Saint Thomas Aquinas was very scholarly, and Saint Thérèse of Lisieux had the nickname "the Little Flower." You and your child can learn about popular saints in picture books, on Catholic websites, and from other resources. Also, your catechist or DRE can direct you to resources on the lives of the saints.

You can use a social story to explain that the Confirmation name chosen is a special or spiritual name. He or she will be called this name by the bishop at Confirmation but almost all other times will still be called by his or her usual name. You can write your own social story or use the one found in the *Adaptive Confirmation Kit* (Loyola Press, 2014).

The Fun Begins

Choosing a sponsor is a personal decision. We know several people who chose their godparents as Confirmation sponsors. Others choose someone else. There is no one right or wrong way to do this. If your child is able, encourage him or her to help choose a sponsor. If he or she is unable to provide input, then trust your instincts.

Consider any special demands that would fall to the sponsor, such as pushing a wheelchair or providing prompts to keep the child on task and where he or she should be at specific parts of the rite. The sponsor should also be aware that placing a hand on the child's shoulder, which is part of the Confirmation ceremony, could be a problem if the child reacts negatively to sensory input such as a light touch. A good way to prevent any problems is to practice this part ahead of time. Try alternating the amount of pressure on the shoulder. It is not uncommon for a light touch to be perceived by the child as unpleasant while a deep touch is tolerated better.

Making It Real

The Rite of Confirmation itself will run longer than a usual Sunday Mass and will most likely be celebrated by the bishop or his representative, with whom your child may be unfamiliar. During the opening procession, Danielle was escorted by her sponsor, Grace, and her father, which made her feel more comfortable. We both sat with Danielle and her sponsor in the pew. The child and sponsor might do well to practice each step of the rite ahead of time. This can be done at home or in church. They can practice walking together, hand on shoulder, and just go over any part of the rite that might be a challenge.

We encourage you to familiarize your child with the bishop. The bishop may ask the Confirmation class questions instead of giving a homily. Invite your child's sponsor to be present as you prepare your child for the Rite in advance. For instance, during Confirmation the bishop traces a cross on the child's forehead with a type of oil called Chrism. Your child might need to get used to the feel of the oil. You can practice using olive oil if you wish. It's also a good time to reinforce the mechanics of blessing oneself and any content that the catechist and DREs feel should be reviewed.

After all the preparation and practice, we were delighted that Danielle's Confirmation went so well. As the bishop said, "She was filled with the Holy Spirit."

Connect to the Word

Do not fear, for I have redeemed you;
I have called you by name, you are mine.

—Isaiah 43:1

Explain to your child that people's names are important. We call people by their names to show we care about them. God cares about us and calls us by name in a special way at Confirmation. Some children with special needs have difficulty with people's names. Until very recently, Danielle was unable to call us by name. With the help of her electronic speech machine, she now addresses each family member. When she does this, joy fills our hearts. We rejoice even more knowing that God, too, is calling us by name!

A Closing Meditation: What's in a Name?

What's in a name? That which we call a rose
by any other name would smell as sweet.

—William Shakespeare

6

Inclusion in Parish Life

We were reading our parish bulletin and saw that the diocese was sponsoring a poster contest for elementary school students. The theme was Right to Life. Shannon was very excited and told us how much she wanted to enter the contest. She said, "Wouldn't it be nice if Danielle could enter it too?" We weren't quite sure how this was going to happen since Danielle cannot write, and her difficulty with fine motor skills, even after years of occupational therapy, makes it hard for her to use a pencil or crayon. But then we remembered how she had used PECS icons for her First Holy Communion invitation and knew that she could do the same for this contest.

Both our girls set about making posters to show their support for right to life. With characteristic enthusiasm, Shannon threw herself into the project. She used a variety of arts and crafts materials along with personal photographs to make her statement. She talked about the value of human life from a young child's perspective. The end result was a sparkly and colorful poster. She was thrilled with the poster and even more thrilled when it was chosen as one of the winning entries in her age category. We were very proud.

Danielle used PECS icons to present the verse from Jeremiah 1:5: "Before I formed you in the womb, I knew you." With our assistance, she was able to cut and paste icons onto a piece of purple oak tag. She added photos of herself at her Baptism, at her First Holy Communion, and as a fourth grader. She was proud of her poster. It was also selected as a winning entry. She was as excited as her sister Shannon.

Both girls received certificates and a monetary prize. Our whole family, including Danielle's grandfather, attended an award luncheon where all the winning posters were on display. The winners were called up one at a time to receive their certificates from a young and very engaging priest from the chancery. He emphasized each child's contribution to the pro-life effort and made all of them feel valued and important. Afterward, he posed for a photograph with each child.

Danielle worked hard on her entry in the diocesan poster contest. No one was happier than she was on the day the priest called her up to receive her award. It just goes to show that with a little creativity, patience, and proper supports, all of God's children can feel like valued members of the faith community and contribute to the life of the Church. We were happy that we helped Danielle take part in this activity. Her poster, the only entry to use PECS, brought attention to the fact that there are children with special needs in our diocese preparing for the sacraments.

Lesson 1: Enhancing Participation at Mass

There's always an opportunity for you to enhance your child's participation in the parish. This doesn't have to be elaborate. There are simple but important things your child can do to help.

For Starters

One of the easiest ways for your child to increase his or her participation in the Mass is to put the family's weekly offering in the collection basket. This is a great way a child can move toward being an active participant with an important job to do.

Begin at home by showing your child that money or a check goes into the envelope. If your child is able, allow him or her to place the money inside and seal the envelope. At the appropriate time during Mass, give the envelope to your child to hold. If he or she is having difficulty, provide hand-over-hand prompts. Make sure the envelope goes into the basket and that your child successfully passes the basket on to the next parishioner in the pew or to the usher. Provide reinforcement such as a hug, deep pressure, or verbal praise.

Danielle puts our envelope in the basket each week. She looks forward to it and smiles at her accomplishment. When other parishioners see Danielle's contribution, they can see that she is both competent and confident in performing an important function of parish life. It took some time to teach her how to do this. It was a process that required consistent repetition and support, but now she can do it without prompting.

The Fun Begins

Your child might want to be an altar server. Not everybody has the interest, desire, or cognitive abilities to do this job, but for those who do it can be very rewarding. Shannon is the only one of our four children who chose to be an altar server. She loved helping at Mass, and it was a pleasure seeing her grow into the role. Children with special needs can be altar servers too, but we recommend that you take steps to ensure your child's success in that role.

Carefully assess whether or not your child can

- follow instructions and remember what he or she needs to do and in the right order.
- adapt to surprises such as a feast day, a Baptism, or a change to the ordinary order of events.
- maintain reverence even if something goes wrong.
- exercise sufficient fine motor skills to perform the required tasks.

Danielle did not have these skills, but many children with special needs do. We know a young man who has a serious neurological condition who became an altar server. One of the challenges he faced was not knowing where to stand on the altar; sometimes he would stand in the same place where the priest was supposed to stand. The priest was able to give him subtle prompts, and certain accommodations were put in place to help indicate where the boy needed to stand.

Another way to support an altar server who needs accommodations is to pair the child with a sibling or friend who is also an altar server. The more experienced server can act as a guide or otherwise familiar presence. It may also be a good idea to practice lighting and carrying altar candles, walking in floor-length robes, carrying the carafes of water and wine if needed, and maintaining a reverent attitude throughout the Mass. Small accommodations like these can make a huge difference in the ability of a child with special needs to participate in such an important activity.

Making It Real

Singing in the choir can be a nice way for a child to participate in parish life. It provides an opportunity to make new friends and contribute to the liturgical experience. As with being an altar server, the church choir is not for everyone. The child must be verbal and able to sing. He or she must have a long enough attention span to sit quietly between songs. There are children with special needs who can do these things.

Being in the church choir has many positives. The structure of the Mass lends itself to predictability and routine. Rehearsal provides opportunity for repetition and practice. Many of the songs will already be familiar to the child. Because choir is a group effort, participation can help develop social skills and friendships. Making beautiful music that uplifts and inspires the congregation can be a source of real joy and accomplishment.

The following are some ways to help a child with special needs who wants to sing in the choir.

- Many choirs have a wooden board with the hymns listed in order and identified by number. This is a natural visual-sequence board that your child can use to stay focused and organized. It can decrease undue anxiety about what happens next.

- Use sticky notes to mark the appropriate locations in the hymnal with the name and number of the song for easy reference. This eliminates frantic searching for the correct song during Mass. These tabs can be color coded, too, if it helps your child.

- Practice using the microphone ahead of time to avoid annoying feedback and volume fluctuation.

- Mark the child's seat with tape or a picture so he or she knows where to sit. If your child tends to encroach on other people's personal space, remind him or her to sit or stand an appropriate distance from the other choir members.

- Your child can invite a friend from the choir to rehearse at home. They can sing songs together around a piano or even a cappella at the kitchen table.

Connect to the Word

Whatever your task, put yourselves into it, as done for the Lord and not for your masters.

—Colossians 3:23

Let your child know that when we help out at church or anywhere else, we are doing God's work. When we approach it from this perspective, we put our hearts and souls into it. Tasks done this way are performed with joy and are rarely burdensome.

Lesson 2: Parish Activities

You can find opportunities for your child to participate in parish and diocesan activities. The amount and type of support needed will vary based on the specific needs of your child, but his or her participation is well worth it. Not only does it provide a chance for your child to serve the church, but it allows parishioners to discover how much the special needs community has to offer.

For Starters

Inclusion opportunities, such as the poster contest, can be found in the parish bulletin, your parish website, and your diocesan newspaper. Through these, we have learned about opportunities for children to participate as altar servers, sing in the children's choir, serve as a greeter, and become members of the parish youth group. We have learned about food and clothing drives and when volunteers are needed to set up coffee and donuts on Fellowship Sundays. Clearly, not every child with special needs will be able to do every activity, but most children can participate in one or more of these with the proper supports and accommodations.

The Fun Begins

Our parish has an event every month called Fellowship Sunday. After Mass the congregation is treated to donuts and coffee, and volunteers are needed to set up and serve. If your parish has something similar, it could be an excellent opportunity for your child to get more involved, as many children with special needs do with minimal support by their parents. In the past, our sons Brendan and Colin have helped out with providing hospitality after such events and after the parish Nativity pageant. So we began to consider how Danielle might help. Not every child will be able to do everything, but each probably will be able to do something. For instance, a child may not be able to pour hot coffee but may be able to pass out paper napkins or donuts. The child may not be able to collect donations but may be able to stand by and assist his or her parent with this task. Your child may be able to greet parishioners. Parents know their children best. Since we worried that Danielle might try to eat the refreshments rather than serve them to others, we gave her a different job. She was able to carry items and clean up with prompts and supervision, so we helped her do these things instead.

Making It Real

If your parish has a Boy Scout or Girl Scout troop, you may wish to consider ways your child with special needs can participate in the program directly or indirectly. Options may include the following:

- Joining the troop as a scout if appropriate
- Joining a special needs scouting troop
- Supporting the activities of a sibling's scout troop

A Family Story

The Boy Scout troop sponsored by our parish has an annual event called Scout Sunday. It is a beautiful way for scouts and their families to participate in the liturgy in various ways including being a greeter, taking up the gifts, and reading from the Word of God. Several Eagle Scout projects have benefitted the parish directly as well. Brendan's project was to develop a special needs resource library for the religious education program; this ultimately became the basis for the *Adaptive First Eucharist Preparation Kit*. Scouting has provided Brendan and our family a way to participate in all kinds of activities and service, and Danielle was able to participate in quite a few of these, including Scout Sunday, Courts of Honor, and fund-raisers. One noteworthy activity that took place in the gathering space of our church was to assemble care packages for the troops serving abroad. All the volunteers present, including Danielle, worked hard to put together these care packages.

Connect to the Word

For just as the body is one and has many members, and all the members of the body, though many, are one body, so it is with Christ. For in the one Spirit we were all baptized into one body—Jews or Greeks, slaves or free—and we were all made to drink of one Spirit.

—1 Corinthians 12:12–13

What does the above passage say about our role as members of the Church? How does this relate to people with disabilities? Why is it important to expand inclusion opportunities for children with special needs?

A Closing Meditation: Setting the World on Fire

If you are what you should be, you will set the whole world on fire!

—Saint Catherine of Siena

Children with special needs can do amazing things just by being themselves. When people see a child with autism or other serious disability participating in the faith community, they may see past the stereotype and begin to recognize the image and likeness of God in all people. A transformation of consciousness can occur that leads to a deeper compassion in all of us. At the same time, the child grows in confidence and ability, recognizes that he or she is part of the same community of faith, and becomes aware of his or her connection to God by being a full member of Christ's body, the Church.

7

Christian Service

On our son Brendan's third birthday, he received a toy Cozy Coupe car with its signature yellow roof and red plastic body. It was the old-fashioned kind that required using your feet to pedal. That little car was built to last. Not only did it stand up to the wear and tear that Brendan subjected it to, but it also survived his three younger siblings. For years it was parked in our garage taking up space and collecting dust. The little coupe and some other toys found a new home when we donated them to a nearby home for women who are pregnant and need a place to stay. Our daughters, Danielle and Shannon, accompanied us there. It was a great chance to teach them compassion and charity.

Perhaps the happiest person we met there was a three-year-old boy named Xavier, who was staying at the home with his mother. Upon seeing the toy car, his eyes lit up, and he said excitedly, "I want that!" Before we knew it, he hopped into the driver's seat. We told Xavier that our son Brendan used to ride in this car, but he is twenty years old now and drives a real car. We all laughed when Xavier innocently asked, "Doesn't he fit in it anymore?" We assured Xavier that Brendan was too big and grown-up to fit in the coupe, but Xavier was just the right size to play with it now.

Donating the toys was a wonderful opportunity to teach both girls about the corporal works of mercy. It was heartwarming to see Danielle carrying her favorite stuffed Care Bear to donate. Shannon summed it up when she said, "I thought I was just going to be a little happy to help, but I feel great!" The rest of us felt pretty great too.

Lesson 1: Works of Mercy

Children get a sense of reward and satisfaction when they know they are helping others. Children with special needs can help too. Parents can teach their children how they can be of service to people in need and that, as followers of Jesus, we are called to respond to such need with compassionate action.

For Starters

Find out about clothing and food drives and other activities that your parish sponsors. Think about ways your family can participate. Help your child with special needs by providing prompts and modifications. Here are a few examples of ways to help your child help others:

- Participate in your parish's monthly food collection. Your child with special needs can help you when you shop for canned goods and other items. He or she can carry your bag of donations into the church. Some children with special needs can help load the bags onto the truck that takes the donated items to the food bank. Explain that the food is going to help people who are hungry.

- Your family may want to participate in a pro-life baby shower or the Christmas giving tree. In these drives your family buys a gift for a specific child. When our boys were young, they always chose to help boys close to their age. Now that our girls are doing the picking, Danielle and Shannon usually choose to help a young girl. Of course they love to buy an outfit or toy for the child and place it under the tree or in the baby-shower basket. We tell each of them how much they are helping.

- Many organizations, such as scout troops, schools, and even stores and supermarkets, sponsor coat drives. When your children donate one of their favorite coats, you can remind them that Jesus told his disciples, "Whoever has two coats must share with anyone who has none; and whoever has food must do likewise" (Luke 3:11).

The Fun Begins

Families often accumulate a lot of items they no longer need. If you can no longer close the closet doors because you have too much stuff, this may be the perfect time to find someone who needs these items more than you do. Also, it's a great time to introduce your child to the art of giving. Over the last few years, as our four children have grown older, it became obvious that we needed to donate many of the items they had outgrown. Luckily, it's easy to find places to donate.

Libraries and schools are often looking for book donations. Shannon takes special pleasure donating books because of her love of reading. She likes it when a book that gave her so much joy goes to another child. Danielle has carried the bag full of books onto the school bus and proudly brought it into her classroom. When someone helps her take the books to the donation basket, she experiences giving firsthand, as well as participating in a meaningful school and community activity.

When we finally got serious about de-cluttering our garage, all the children including Danielle assisted in some way. Items were sorted into piles to donate. One of these piles contained baseball and soccer cleats that we had accumulated over the years. Danielle put the cleats into a box and drove with us to the Cleats for Kids donation site located at a nearby practice field. The young men who were in charge of receiving the donations were amazed as we filled the container with so many pairs of cleats. We were happy that our garage was cleaner and that the cleats would be put to good use, and Danielle had a smile on her face as we drove home.

In addition to the cleats, we donated several bikes that the children had outgrown. We brought these to a Christian organization that refurbishes the bikes to make them look almost new. They work throughout the year on this, and on Christmas morning they deliver over 800 bikes to children in Camden, New Jersey. Again, Danielle accompanied us and wheeled over a small pink bike with a basket and streamers. We asked one of the men loading the bikes onto a big truck, "What is the name of your organization?" He answered, "Jesus." And with that, we returned to our car feeling as if we had done something good. We believe Danielle felt this too. She gets it.

Making It Real

If you are having trouble finding ways your child with special needs can be of service to others, consider donating his or her eyeglasses that are no longer used to the Lions Club Recycle for Sight program. Eyeglasses are collected and refurbished for people in developing countries who may lack access to prescription eyewear. Danielle has been wearing glasses since preschool, so she has accumulated quite a few pairs. The glasses that Danielle has outgrown are now helping other children see clearly.

Your child can donate her hair to the organization Locks of Love, which uses the hair to make wigs for cancer patients. Growing your hair long may not seem like a big deal; however, for children who have sensory issues from autism or other disabilities, combing out tangles in long hair may not be easy. Haircuts can be difficult too. When Danielle was younger, she had very long, thick blonde hair. Whenever she got her hair cut, she would try to block the scissors with her hands, wiggle in her seat, and take off the cape. So for her to grow her hair and have it cut off to be donated involved some sacrifice. We did our best to explain to Danielle that her hair was beautiful and that she was going to cut some of it off to give to a child who needed hair. We kept it simple. At last, when her hair was long enough, we said a prayer for a quick and easy haircut. Thankfully, she allowed our friend and hairdresser Sharon to comb it straight and cut off a ten-inch ponytail. Danielle held the long lock of hair in her hands and seemed quite pleased with her accomplishment.

A Family Story

This gift of hair reminded us of the famous story "The Gift of the Magi" by O. Henry. Mercedes's father loved this story and would read it to his family every Christmas. The story involves a young couple who each sell their most treasured possession to get money to purchase a special gift for the other. Della has long, beautiful hair, which she sells to buy a gold watch chain for her husband, Jim. Jim, however, has already sold his watch to buy combs for Della's beautiful hair. Since this is a famous story and a family favorite, we know our children will hear it many more times throughout their lives. We hope they will recall their grandfather's love for this poignant story and relate it to their sister's donation to Locks of Love. Our Danielle in her own way gave as beautiful and precious a gift. Further, this story demonstrates that if you are creative, you can find opportunities for your child to give of himself or herself in service to others.

Connect to the Word

"Then the king will say to those at his right hand, 'Come, you that are blessed by my Father, inherit the kingdom prepared for you from the foundation of the world; for I was hungry and you gave me food, I was thirsty and you gave me something to drink, I was a stranger and you welcomed me, I was naked and you gave me clothing, I was sick and you took care of me, I was in prison and you visited me.' Then the righteous will answer him, 'Lord, when was it that we saw you hungry and gave you food, or thirsty and gave you something to drink? And when was it that we saw you a stranger and welcomed you, or naked and gave you clothing? And when was it that we saw you sick or in prison and visited you?' And the king will answer them, 'Truly I tell you, just as you did it to one of the least of these who are members of my family, you did it to me.'"

—Matthew 25:34–40

Lesson 2: More Works of Mercy

When you're raising a child with a serious disability, getting involved in the community might be the last thing you feel like doing. There are so many demands on your time, and you feel overwhelmed and in need of a break yourself. You may worry about your child's ability to behave appropriately at community events. But getting out and involved in community projects and events may be just what you and your child need.

For Starters

When families are touched by something as life changing as autism or other disability, they can feel powerless. How do you respond to something that turns your life upside down? One good way is to help focus public attention on the issue and help fund research that may lead to effective treatments or even a cure. Participating in a charity walk or run does both. You can find a walk to help raise funds and increase public awareness to help those who have breast cancer, autism, multiple sclerosis, and many other conditions.

Our family has participated in a walk for autism. We have walked with Danielle's school team as well as forming our own Danielle's Dream Team. These walks are a fun family and community activity that benefits a good cause. Danielle loves to walk and even runs ahead of the rest of us. Fortunately, her brother Colin is always fast enough to catch her before she gets too far ahead. This type of event may work well for your family. You can easily adapt it to the needs of your child; you can walk at your own pace, take a rest break, or even take a shortcut. Afterward, you can visit the information booths to learn about the latest findings in research. Once we even met Miss New Jersey, who gave both girls (and Dave) an autographed picture!

The Fun Begins

School-related charitable events are another way for your child to serve the community. Many schools participate in activities that raise money for worthy causes. These are widely publicized by the school via literature sent home in your child's backpack or on school-district websites.

The Jump Rope for Heart is a fund-raising effort in which elementary and middle-school children jump rope to raise money to help the American Heart Association. It's a lot of fun because the child participates in this activity with his or her peers. The children practice jumping rope in gym class. The activity can be adapted to fit your child's skill level. For children who enjoy physical activities, this is a win-win situation. Since jumping rope is a common schoolyard pastime, learning how to do it can be an important social skill for your child. Another great school activity is Pennies for Patients, sponsored by the Leukemia and Lymphoma Society. Children bring their loose change to school and contribute to their classroom's donation. Sometimes classrooms compete against each other to see which class can raise the most money.

Making It Real

You can also find opportunities for Christian service within your own family. Grandparents find visits from their grandchildren to be particularly welcomed. Brendan, Colin, Danielle, and Shannon brought great joy to their grandparents just by their presence. The children would fill in their grandparents on their school projects, sporting events, and anything else that was going on in their lives. Danielle was able to use photographs to show what was going on in her life, such as participating in Special Olympics. When their grandfather would come over for dinner each week, the children loved to help by bringing in the groceries, setting the table, and cleaning up after dinner. Danielle participated in these activities with prompts and assistance. When our children would visit their grandmother, they would help her by bringing things she asked for, watering the flowers, and cleaning up around the house. Helping the elderly is not limited to one's grandparents. Neighbors and friends of the family may enjoy a visit too. It is a good idea for parents to accompany their children on these visits and to assist as needed, especially their children who have special needs.

Connect to the Word

Religion that is pure and undefiled before God, the Father, is this: to care for orphans and widows in their distress.

—James 1:27

Explain to your child how much God wants us to help others, especially people who are elderly and infirm. Children with special needs should be encouraged to help siblings, parents, grandparents, and other elders.

A Closing Meditation: On Compassion

If you want others to be happy, practice compassion. If you want to be happy, practice compassion.

—The Dalai Lama

8

Joyous Moments and How to Celebrate Them

Our family loves to decorate the house and make it festive during the holiday season. Who doesn't love putting up a Christmas tree, Advent wreath, and crèche? Decorating is a chance for everyone to get involved. In preparing for Christmas, the excitement begins to mount as soon as Thanksgiving is over. Our children have always looked forward to putting up the Christmas tree. Our living room has a cathedral ceiling, and one year the boys chose a really big tree that would almost touch the ceiling. When we were finished putting it up, we all admired the beautiful tree and its decorations. We had no idea that all our work would be undone in a matter of seconds.

Danielle decided to reach up and grab a dangling ornament. This looked to her like the perfect item to shake and rattle. The dangling ornament was just too inviting. She grabbed it hard and pulled the tree over. Crash! The fallen Christmas tree lay on its side in our living room. Danielle was laughing. Shannon was crying. The boys were mad. We were frustrated, and everyone was sick and tired of autism. It all seemed so senseless. We felt particularly bad for our children since they had put so much effort into it and were so proud of the result. We swept up the broken remains of our favorite ornaments, and we all wondered why such a thing had to happen. After all, this was supposed to be a season of hope and joy!

Celebrations are important in everyone's life. Families of children with special needs deserve to celebrate Christmas and other such events without worrying that the tree will come crashing down. The lessons in this chapter will revolve around how to teach children with special needs about two joyous moments in life, Baptisms and Christmas.

Lesson 1: Baptisms

There is nothing more joyous than the birth of a new baby. Our family experienced this joy upon hearing the news of the birth of our great-nephew Jackson Henry. He was born in Florida, hundreds of miles away from New Jersey, but when his picture arrived via text messaging, there were oohs and aahs and a fierce debate over which family member he most resembled. We brought Danielle into the excitement by signing "baby" and showing her the picture of Jackson and his parents, Kimberly and Jack. Babies are meant to be celebrated, especially upon their christening day when they are welcomed into the Church.

For Starters

Many children on the autism spectrum have a narrow range of interests. If you can find some way to work this interest into the lesson, there's a good chance your child will attend to what you are trying to teach. For example, if your child is interested in dolls, dolls can be a great way to prepare a child with special needs to celebrate a family Baptism. Dolls are fun, visual, easily available, and they can be motivating and reinforcing. Although Danielle did not play with dolls in a traditional way due to her autism, she did show interest in one particular doll. This doll had a variety of outfits including a christening dress. On the day that Shannon was baptized, Father Mike, a family friend, used the doll to explain the Baptism rite to all the young children present. We can still see Father Mike holding up the doll and saying, "When a baby is baptized, the priest pours water on his or her head and says 'I baptize you in the name of the Father and of the Son and of the Holy Spirit.'"

In preparation for an upcoming baptismal celebration, find a doll, puppet, or action figure that your child is interested in and use it to model what will happen during the ceremony. In our case, the doll bore a natural resemblance to the baby being baptized and even had a christening gown. However, if this sort of doll isn't of interest to your child, find something that is, even if it's an action figure or a stuffed animal. What's important is your child's interest, not the object itself.

Explain that when babies are young, they are baptized and become part of the Church family. Mention to your child that he or she will be welcoming a new sibling, cousin, or whatever the case may be into the Church. At the sink, tub, or another appropriate place, explain that when a baby is baptized, the priest pours water on the baby's forehead and says, "I baptize you in the name of the Father and of the Son and of the Holy Spirit." You can use the Bless Yourself puzzle from the *Adaptive First Eucharist Preparation Kit* to help sequence the Sign of the Cross.

The Fun Begins

A Baptism, whether private or incorporated into the Sunday Mass, can be a teaching opportunity. It's a great time to explain the role of godparents. You can use this occasion to talk to your children about their own christening and their own godparents. Some children may not know they have godparents. Perhaps their godparents will be present. Perhaps their godparents are the mother or father of the baby being baptized. Celebrations bring people together and provide a natural vehicle whereby families can reminisce and children can become reacquainted with their godparents.

Making It Real

Explain to your child that all of us are part of the Church family and that the new baby is part of this family too. Your family may find itself celebrating a Baptism in several different ways. The Baptism might be held after Mass, with a group of babies receiving the sacrament together. Alternatively, a Baptism might be private, especially if a friend or family member is a priest. Since this was the case for our children, we were able to add special touches to the celebrations. At other times a baby will be baptized during the regular Sunday Mass. Occasionally, our pastor does this because it gives the parish a chance to welcome the baby as a new member of the Christian community. If this is the case, you may wish to prepare your child in advance since there might be a larger crowd with more noise and the order of the proceedings will be different from an ordinary Mass. Some children may become upset or perplexed when what happens during the Baptism service deviates from what typically occurs during Mass. Gently explain beforehand and remind your child as necessary that a baby is being baptized so church will be a little different than usual. As it is important to maintain a proper level of reverence during the ceremony, this is a good opportunity to review and practice reverent behaviors, such as blessing oneself and sitting quietly.

Lastly, an adult may be baptized as part of the Rite of Christian Initiation of Adults (RCIA). When this happened at our church, Danielle actively participated by holding her hand out with the rest of the parish to welcome the young adults who were being baptized into the faith. This moment was a heartwarming surprise because it was so natural and spontaneous, which we attributed to the years of bringing Danielle to church and exposing her to the beautiful liturgy, prayers, and sacraments of our faith, her faith. We could see that Danielle is truly a member of the Church.

The array of variation in baptismal settings might be confusing to your child, particularly if he or she has special needs. If this is a problem, consider writing a social story in which such variations are presented and resolved with a line that goes something like this: "That's okay, it's still Baptism."

Connect to the Word

In those days Jesus came from Nazareth of Galilee and was baptized by John in the Jordan. And just as he was coming up out of the water, he saw the heavens torn apart and the Spirit descending like a dove on him. And a voice came from heaven, "You are my Son, the Beloved; with you I am well pleased."

—Mark 1:9–11

This is a very picturesque passage in the Gospel of Mark where Jesus is baptized by John the Baptist and receives the Holy Spirit in the form of a dove. Many illustrated children's Bibles present this story. Explain to your child how Jesus was baptized and how the Spirit descended on him. Explain how God the Father told Jesus that he was his Son and that he loved him. Explain to your child how much you love him or her and that he or she is loved by God too.

Lesson 2: Christmas

Christmas can be a stressful time for families of children with special needs. Ordinary routines are rearranged or suspended. Suddenly there's a tree growing out of your living room floor! The season can be hectic with shopping, parties, and guests. The true meaning of Christmas can often be forgotten. This lesson involves ways to teach children with special needs about the meaning of Christmas and how to celebrate it with joy and reverence.

For Starters

Your family can make some minor adjustments to minimize the chance of damage to ornaments and decorations during the Christmas season. Refrain from putting irreplaceable and breakable ornaments on the tree. This includes dangling ornaments and garland. We've chosen, instead, to give each child two boxes—one to keep their breakable, irreplaceable ornaments and a second for ornaments that are more durable. When the tree goes up, each child puts only the second set of ornaments on the tree. The more fragile ornaments are kept safe for when the children are grown and have their own Christmas trees in their own homes. We develop each collection by adding a new ornament annually that depicts a milestone or something special that happened that year.

Clear the mantle of garlands, candles, and dangling stockings. Hang your stockings on a stairway bannister or elsewhere, out of easy reach. Consider temporarily putting your family's more expensive and fragile crèche in storage. Have your children make a homemade crèche out of inexpensive craft materials and display it on the mantle instead.

You may find that these changes need only be temporary measures. Often when a child with special needs loses access or the opportunity to engage in a maladaptive behavior, the behavior loses its strength.

When you reintroduce more fragile or expensive ornaments later, you may find that your child tolerates them without any problem. This happened to us. Dave's mother passed away a few years after we cleared our home of expensive and breakable items. Tentatively, we placed one of the ornaments from her tree onto ours. From that Christmas on, Danielle no longer showed any interest in pulling down the stockings, crèche, ornaments, or tree. We were able to display the crèche we had put away and even have started hanging a few more fragile ornaments on the tree. Christmas has gotten easier. We make sure Grandma's ornament is the first ornament we hang on the tree each year.

The Fun Begins

What better way to prepare for the birth of the infant Jesus than by putting your family's artistic talents to work making an Advent wreath? Last year our parish hosted a workshop for families to make and decorate Advent wreaths. Shannon helped Danielle by providing prompts and giving her an opportunity to imitate her actions. The finished product looked great! Once home we gathered around the wreath. Danielle blessed herself as our family said a brief prayer then lit the appropriate candle.

We recommend that you give this a try at home. Gather evergreens, pine cones, and holly berries from outdoors, or obtain garlands and ribbons from a craft store. Look for Advent candles in a religious supply store or gift shop. Please remember to provide proper safety precautions and supervision when lighting the candles.

Making It Real

For people of faith, the central focus of Christmas is the Nativity of Our Lord Jesus Christ. There are plenty of ways to highlight this mystery of faith, including visiting a crèche and participating in a Christmas pageant. Both options can appeal to the learning styles of children with special needs because they present the birth of Jesus in an immediate, visual, and concrete way.

Attend a Crèche Saint Francis of Assisi is credited with inventing the crèche, a reenactment of the story of Jesus' birth in the stable using live animals placed around the crib of the infant Jesus. Animals and babies are naturally appealing, and the Nativity story is one of the most cherished and repeated stories in Christianity and the culture at large. We attend a living Nativity in a neighboring town that uses members of the congregation, local farm animals, and stage sets to portray not only the birth of Jesus but also scenes from his public ministry. All the senses are engaged, from seeing the heavenly host appearing in the sky above the heads of frightened shepherds, to hearing the merchants in the village of Bethlehem and touching the wool coat of lambs and sheep. For many winters now our family has put on warm clothes and enjoyed the outdoor event as if we were actually living the story. Danielle looks on with as much enthusiasm and fascination as any of us. At the end of the presentation, everyone is invited to enjoy cookies and hot chocolate.

Children with special needs may take a little time to get used to events like this with crowds, long lines, and noise. You may opt to go early in the season when there are smaller crowds and only stay as long as your child can tolerate. You might prefer a less elaborate crèche, which can often be found in small churchyards across the country. Also, many churches place a crèche with statues of the baby Jesus, Mary, and Joseph near the altar during Advent and Christmas. Of course there are no live animals indoors, but there may be statues of an ox or lamb in the scene. Take your child to visit the crib after Mass, so he or she can experience the scene up close.

The Christmas Pageant Many parishes and religious schools present Christmas pageants. Children dress in costumes and sing songs. Children play angels, shepherds, wise men, Joseph, and

Mary. As with a live crèche, Christmas pageants are concrete, visual, and fun for all.

Christmas Parties Holiday parties can be stressful for a family or a child with special needs. One good way to minimize stress is to find a party where the people there understand what you're going through. We attend an annual Christmas party sponsored by the Elks Club for children with disabilities. In addition, we attend a children's Christmas party sponsored by the Knights of Columbus. Mercedes's father was a past Grand Knight of this council, and we have attended this party for years. At parties like these, our family is able to relax and celebrate.

Connect to the Word

In that region there were shepherds living in the fields, keeping watch over their flock by night. Then an angel of the Lord stood before them, and the glory of the Lord shone around them, and they were terrified. But the angel said to them, "Do not be afraid; for see—I am bringing you good news of great joy for all the people: to you is born this day in the city of David a Savior, who is the Messiah, the Lord. This will be a sign for you: you will find a child wrapped in bands of cloth and lying in a manger." And suddenly there was with the angel a multitude of the heavenly host, praising God and saying,

"Glory to God in the highest heaven,
and on earth peace among those whom he favors!"
—Luke 2:8–14

A Closing Meditation: Seek God

Seek God and you will find him;
Seek him in everything and you will find him in
    everything;
Seek him always and you will find him always.

—Saint Vincent Pallotti

Celebrations are our opportunity to seek God in our daily lives and relationships. When we celebrate joyous occasions with others, we are in fact affirming the presence of God in the world, the mystery of the Incarnation and of Christ's Resurrection and redemption. Parents of children with special needs and their families do not have to stop celebrating.

9

To Everything There Is a Season

One Easter, shortly after the death of Danielle's grandmother, Danielle and Dave decided to get some fresh air and take a walk outside. Before her grandmother died, Danielle liked to walk the half mile with her dad from her uncle's house to the small ranch-style home where Grandma lived. Today, however, Dave seemed to be taking a different route. Danielle broke away and started to run in the direction of her grandma's house. When she arrived, she stood outside the house expectantly. When Dave finally caught up with her, he said sadly, "I'm sorry, Danielle, but Grandma lives in heaven now."

This chapter deals with the difficult task of explaining death and loss to children with special needs. Danielle and her siblings have lost all four of their grandparents. Death is a complicated mystery to all of us, especially to children. For a child with a developmental disability, death can be even more mysterious and difficult to understand.

Three years later, our children lost their final grandparent, their Poppy, Mercedes's father. Each of our children felt the void. Their grandparents were special individuals in the lives of our children. These special people were always in their corner, always relishing in their accomplishments. They took pride in attending their grandchildren's activities and events. When they died, their absence left a deep void indeed.

Lesson 1: Grief and Loss

Blessed Teresa of Calcutta said, "Death is nothing else but going home to God, the bond of love will be unbroken for all eternity." It is comforting to know that our loved ones are happy in the presence of God. But as we have all experienced, grief is difficult for those of us who remain. Children with special needs may have even more difficulty understanding loss and grief because of language and cognitive impairments. The rituals of our faith, especially the funeral, can help.

For Starters

The unexpected death of Mercedes's mother was our children's first experience with loss. Our boys were quite young. Brendan was three, and Colin was one. When she passed away, the question arose as to whether or not they should attend her funeral. While the undertaker suggested that we allow them to attend so that they would have a measure of closure, we decided against it. We thought that it would be too hard of a day. Since our boys were so young, we believe this was the correct decision. However, when the remaining grandparents died, our children did attend the funeral services. This is a very personal decision. There is no right or wrong answer.

If you do decide to have your child attend a funeral, there are some things you can do to ease the anxiety around this experience.

Take your child's attention span and tolerance into account. You may wish to bring your child into the church when the viewing is almost over so it won't be too long for her. We walked Danielle past the open coffin and selected a seat just prior to the start of the funeral Mass. Just as when attending Sunday Mass, select a seat that will make it easy for you to exit with your child if needed.

Find a way for your child to participate if possible. This may be as simple as accompanying cousins and siblings as they bring the gifts to the altar. Depending on cognition and behavior, your child may be able to participate in other ways during the Mass, such as being a reader, singing, or even being an altar server. You may wish to escort your child and provide prompts as needed.

Let's Begin

Even if your children have never experienced the loss of a grandparent or other loved one, they may have lost a beloved pet. They may be very sad and need to process their grief. When our daughter Shannon was ten, she lost her guinea pig, Lucky. She was very upset. A few days after Lucky's death, Shannon wrote an account of the experience. We are including the piece in its entirety because it tells what we did to help Shannon through her grief.

> IN MEMORY OF LUCKY THE GUINEA PIG
> By Shannon Rizzo
> "Shannon, Lucky died," said my father as sympathy filled his eyes. I thought my heart had stopped beating. I burst out in tears. "Lucky is my best friend. I had her for five years. She was getting better," I wept. "Honey, we tried, she was just too old." Two hours later we had a funeral. My dad dug a hole and we lowered her in. As we buried her we said a prayer to God to ask him for Lucky to be well loved. Then we said a prayer to St. Francis, the saint of animals. I made a tombstone that read "Lucky Beasty Rizzo 2006–2011." Then we went inside and my mother called the head of the altar servers to get a substitute for me since it was a Sunday. I cried all morning. The next day when I came home from school my mom told me her friend suggested that we get a bunny rabbit. Maybe we will get one, but it will never replace Lucky.

Shannon does not have a disability, but some of the things she wrote about—having a funeral in the backyard with prayers to God and Saint Francis, making a tombstone out of a large pebble, and getting a new pet after a respectable time has elapsed—can provide a direct and intuitive avenue for healing. Such avenues may connect in a deeper way than language-based explanations.

Making It Real

As we mentioned above, people with developmental disabilities may have a hard time understanding death and what it means. We know an adult resident of a developmental center who lost his mother about ten years ago. Although he was told of his mother's death at the time, he frequently asks, "Mommy coming?" His anxiety can build to a high level when he searches for her.

One way to help a person with a disability accept the death of a loved one is to visit the gravesite occasionally. You can leave flowers or other items such as shamrocks on St. Patrick's Day, wreathes and grave blankets on Christmas, and flags on Memorial Day. Your child with special needs can help with the selection and place these items reverently at the grave. End with a brief prayer such as the Our Father or Hail Mary, and in the car tell stories to remember your loved ones. Our family does all these things. Danielle comes with us and can be seen smiling as she brings flowers to adorn the gravesite. In this way she maintains a real connection with her deceased grandparents.

Connect to the Word

"For everything there is a season, and a time for every
   matter under heaven:
a time to be born, and a time to die;
a time to plant, and a time to pluck up what is planted;
a time to kill, and a time to heal;
a time to break down, and a time to build up;
a time to weep, and a time to laugh;
a time to mourn, and a time to dance."
—Ecclesiastes 3:1–4

Lesson 2: Triggering Happy Memories

Our ordinary lives contain opportunities for us to remember our deceased loved ones. These opportunities may arise spontaneously or intentionally. We can use these moments to remember and honor those who are no longer with us and to experience in a real way the love we still have for them.

For Starters

Certain tangible objects or experiences may cause us to remember a loved one who has passed. Most of us are familiar with the feeling. We come across an everyday object, such as a postage stamp or a paintbrush, and we are transported as it were into the presence of our deceased loved one. We do this by association. The important thing is to pay attention to this while it is happening and to use it as a conscious opportunity for remembrance.

Dave's father, Vince, used to tell us that his own mother loved the song "Ave Maria." She once told him that no wedding was complete unless the "Ave Maria" was sung or played at least once during the festivities. We made sure it was sung at our wedding, and Vince remarked how it made him remember his mother. We have shared this story and their grandfather's love of the song with our own children. Every time we hear it played at Mass or elsewhere, we use this as an opportunity to remember Grandpa Vince.

Think about the opportunities for remembrance in your life. Perhaps a loved one left behind an item that can be given to your child for everyday use. Associations play an important part in the learning style of children with autism and related disabilities. You may find that your child responds well to such an approach. Remind your child that the item belonged to the loved one. Tell stories that will help your child remember his or her loved one fondly.

A Family Story

Danielle received her Grandma Ellen's adult-sized tricycle. She rides it all around the neighborhood. We refer to it as "Grandma's Trike" to remind Danielle that the tricycle came from her grandmother. Every ride is an opportunity to tell stories about Grandma Ellen and how much she loved Danielle. She seems quite happy to hear these stories.

The Fun Begins

Throughout the year, certain days stand out as clear opportunities to remember loved ones. Birthdays, anniversaries, Mother's Day, Father's Day, and holidays are such days.

One beautiful and easy way to remember your loved ones is to have a Mass said for them on their special day and to attend this Mass with your family. Your family might bring up the gifts during the memorial Mass. Some parishes offer the opportunity to bring flowers to adorn the altar on Mother's Day, Father's Day, Easter, and Christmas.

Find special days and build associations between that day and your loved one, and pass on these associations to your children whenever possible. Mercedes's father, John, was heavily involved in the Knights of Columbus. For many years he organized and participated in his council's annual Tootsie Roll Drive, which benefits people with developmental disabilities. Now when Tootsie Roll Drive weekend comes around and our children see the Knights conducting their drive, it brings a smile to their faces and they reach into their pockets to donate. They remember their Poppy when they do this. We give Danielle money to put in the collection and remind her that Poppy helped with this drive every year.

Making It Real

Mercedes's mother used to babysit Brendan and Colin when they were toddlers. They called her Nana. When she died suddenly, the boys, even though they were little, would ask for her every day. We told them that she was in heaven. Every day they would ask questions like, "Where is heaven? Can we go to heaven too? When is Nana coming back? Why did Nana go to heaven?" These aspects of death can be very confusing and troubling to young children and those with special needs.

Mercedes sat down with the boys, and together they wrote a children's story called "My Nana Went to Heaven." It was very helpful to them. It explained their Nana's death in terms they could understand. Looking back, we now see how this worked for the boys in a similar way as a social story works for children with special needs. Here is the story we wrote about Nana.

My Nana Went to Heaven
My name is Brendan. I have a Nana, her name is Betty.

She is a very nice Nana. She takes good care of me and my brother Colin. She calls us both "Pudding Pie."

Colin and I love to go to Nana and Poppy's house.

Nana reads us many, many books. Colin and I really like the "bear books."

Nana always has good things to eat at her house. We like cookies and pizza, yum, yum!

Sometimes Nana and Poppy take us to the park across the street, and we swing on the swings. We just love to go there! On other days we drive in Poppy's blue car to different parks to play. When it's windy outside Nana says:

"Oh my goodness, it is time to go home."

One day, Nana got sick. We wanted her to feel better. Poppy took her to the doctor's. My Nana did not feel better. She had to go to the hospital. The ambulance took her to the hospital. We had never seen an ambulance before.

Mommy said that Nana died and went to heaven. We did not understand what that meant. We just wanted our Nana to come home again.

Mommy said that God could make Nana feel better, so Nana went to heaven to live with God. Mommy said that Nana did not want to leave Colin and me, but she had to so that she could feel better. I miss my Nana very much and so does Colin. Colin and I felt very sad. We didn't want our Nana to die. We wanted to go to heaven too. Mommy said that we could not go to Heaven, that we had to stay and take care of her, Poppy, and Daddy. Mommy said that when we miss Nana we can look at all of her pictures. I know that my Nana can see me from Heaven. She is high up in the sky with God and the angels. Sometimes at night, Colin and I look up at the sky for Nana's star. We know that Nana blinks her star and says "Hi Pudding Pie, I miss you, too."

The End

Connect to the Word

"Thus says the Lord . . . I have heard your prayer, I have seen your tears."

—Isaiah 38:5

A Closing Meditation: Life Is to Be Lived

We have a finite amount of time, whether short or long. It doesn't matter. Life is to be lived.

—Randy Pausch, *The Last Lecture*

10

Marriage and Self-Care

On a particular Sunday we decided to go to an earlier Mass than usual. For the first time in quite a while Shannon had no altar service, choir, or religious education commitments that would make it necessary for us to attend the later Mass. Going earlier would allow us to have the remainder of the day wide open. Danielle had slept poorly the night before and had been up well past her normal bedtime. We decided to do something we rarely had been able to do before—allow her to sleep in while her older brothers stayed home with her.

Taking this opportunity for some private worship was long overdue. Even though Danielle had been doing very well attending Mass each week with us, we looked forward to this chance when the two of us would be able to completely relax and enjoy the spiritual refreshment that Mass offers. There are always good days and bad days when dealing with autism; you just never know which day it is going to be.

For many years we were limited in our ability to leave Danielle in her siblings' care. They were younger, and her need for supervision was much higher. However, the boys were now adults and Danielle had made a lot of progress so we decided to indulge in a little self-care and attend Mass, just the two of us.

The first thing that we noticed was that there were no restrictions on where we chose to sit. We had gotten into the habit of sitting in only one or two pews to build a familiar routine for Danielle, but now we could sit on the center aisle near the front of the church. Additionally, we sat next to each other. For the last twenty years, we always had one of our children between us.

It was even possible to kneel in prayer with our eyes closed before the entrance hymn and after receiving Communion. It felt good to be able to devote our full attention to the liturgy and to listen for God's voice in the space between each breath. We felt our muscles relaxing and our thoughts becoming clear and still. This level of prayerfulness is difficult to attain when you're busy assisting children in the pew. As children grow older, this ability to pray the Mass deeply becomes more available to parents. It takes longer for this to happen when you are the parent of a child with special needs. Danielle's behavior at Mass had gotten so much better, but it sure felt good to pray with carefree abandon this Sunday.

It happened to be the monthly Fellowship Sunday. When Mass ended, we had the opportunity to have a leisurely cup of coffee and conversation with other parishioners. We went home renewed and refreshed.

We share this story because it is necessary to look for small opportunities such as this to carve out sacred space. Sometimes parents of children with special needs neglect to do this because they are overwhelmed attending to the necessary demands of raising their children. Yet for your own sake, try to take notice of such opportunities when they do arise, to make time and space for your marriage, to be a couple and not just parents. This chapter will focus on parental self-care and enjoying a happy marriage while raising children, including those with special needs.

Lesson 1: "And I Will Give You Rest"

Raising a child with special needs is stressful. It's important that parents find time for personal renewal so that they have sufficient reserve to care for their child. Just as a flight attendant instructs you to place your mask on first in the event of a sudden drop of air pressure and then attend to your child, parents of children with disabilities need to take care of themselves.

In the beginning of our slow dance with autism, our time for personal renewal was at a minimum. Looking back now, we wish we'd made it a higher priority. But over time we learned the value of self-care and how important it was to maintain time for personal pursuits, hobbies, and friends.

Do Something That Matches Your Interests

Danielle was eligible for the preschool program for children with disabilities when she turned three years old. Even though she only attended a few hours each day, it gave Mercedes a welcome break. She joined a local mother's group that met at a nearby church once a month. It was a fun opportunity to meet other moms with young children, and she enjoyed the time out. There were great refreshments and worthwhile speakers on topics of interest to young parents. The best part of all was that Mercedes could attend while Danielle was in preschool. The group provided a little boost where Mercedes was temporarily lifted out of the autism world, with its seemingly endless list of therapies and medical appointments. She enjoyed feeling like a "regular mom" when she was there.

David got a little break too. He was able to attend a poetry group that met once a month at a local bookstore in the early evening. Meeting with the group gave him an opportunity to pursue his love of poetry, write poems, and share them with other local poets. Some of the poems allowed him to work through and express what he was feeling as the father of a child with a severe disability. It was very therapeutic for him.

These activities were our way of carving out sacred space. Although the groups met only once per month, it was enough to help us maintain our sanity during some very rough times. Obviously, these activities were centered on our personal interests. We're not saying you need to attend a poetry group or a mother's group, but we are suggesting that you try to find something that matches your personality and interests and then do it. Also, when one parent is having a particularly rough day, the other parent can take the children for an hour or so to give the stressed-out parent a chance to get out of the house and blow off some steam.

Find a Way to Get Out by Yourself

At least once a year, indulge yourself by attending a fashion show, sporting event, party, or something similar. Make it special. Remember, this event is just for you. Choose something you would have attended before you became the parent of a child with special needs. Do it even if you think you're too busy to attend.

When our sons were in high school, the parent association ran an annual fashion show. The event was a great evening out at a fancy hotel and included dinner. Mercedes looked forward to going each year. The show always included a huge raffle with great prizes. One year Mercedes won a big prize, which included a pair of tickets to see the Philadelphia Flyers hockey team. The seats were great—in a corporate suite with lots of food and a spectacular view. Dave and Colin are sports fans, so Mercedes was happy that she had won such a fantastic prize. God was smiling on us that day because both of us got a much-needed evening out. It was important, too, because it gave Dave a chance to spend time with Colin, who still recalls with great fondness watching that game with his dad.

Marriage and Self-Care   111

Find a Support Group

We were very fortunate to find a group called Parents of Autistic Children Together (PACT). One of the nice things about this group was that it offered many family outings. What we loved about the PACT outings was that everyone there understood what we were going through. We could relax and have a good time. There was no concern about unwanted stares from people who were offended or shocked by autistic behaviors. We felt that we were understood and supported by a community. It is most definitely a form of self-care to put yourself in a nurturing environment with people whom you could trust to affirm you. One great annual event that PACT sponsors is a trip to a Philadelphia Phillies baseball game. It has become a favorite family activity. Just because you have a child with a disability doesn't mean that you have to give up doing the things you enjoy.

Rekindle an Old Hobby

Dave enjoyed acting in plays in school and in community theater when he was younger. After a twenty-year hiatus from being on stage, he appeared in a community theater production of the musical *Footloose*. What made this even more fun was that Shannon has developed an interest in theater as well, and she appeared in the production with him. The time commitment for rehearsals was challenging, so we limit it to one play a year. By attending the play on a less crowded night and with careful seat selection, Mercedes and Danielle were able to go and enjoy the show.

Find an Annual Respite to Relax and Recharge

We did not do this until Danielle turned thirteen. Our local Elks Club sponsors a weeklong summer camp in the mountains for children with special needs. The camp offers recreational and social activities that promote independence, friendships, and confidence. Although we were aware of this program when Danielle was younger and had heard glowing reports from other parents, we were uneasy about her being away from us for a whole week. However, we decided to send her one very hot summer day when we reached our absolute limit. We were sitting on the porch when Danielle decided to go back inside. We thought she had gone into the family room where the boys were watching TV. This proved to be a big mistake because instead of going to the family room as she usually did, she ran up the stairs to the bathroom. A few minutes later, Colin came outside to inform us that water was leaking through the dining room ceiling. Danielle had turned on the bathroom sink, and now the water was overflowing. The water ran into the crystal chandelier that hung from the ceiling. The expensive chandelier had to be replaced along with part of the ceiling. That day we called the camp and put her on the list. We needed a break.

We wish we had taken advantage of it sooner. Elks Camp Moore has been called "the miracle on the mountain." It provides great fun for the campers and a much-needed respite for parents. It turned out to be an exceptional experience for Danielle. She was happy to be there and well cared for. We were grateful to the Elks Club for their generosity since the program is free of charge. There may be similar programs in your area, and we recommend looking into it.

A Family Story

While Danielle was at camp, we were able to spend a few nights in New York City. We stood outside at Rockefeller Center for the taping of the *Today Show* and got to be in the studio audience for *Live with Kelly!* We went to Central Park and took a carriage ride together. We had a great time seeing the sights and enjoying the restaurants. Even though Dave is a native New Yorker, he enjoyed being a tourist on that trip. It was a bit nerve-racking to leave Danielle in someone else's care. We felt the same as we did the first time we left our oldest child, Brendan, with a babysitter. We wondered if Danielle was okay, and we regularly checked our cell phones for messages. When we were near St. Patrick's Cathedral, we stopped inside to say a prayer and put it in God's hands. This allowed us to relax and put the cell phones away. If you can arrange to get away, if even for an overnight, it will work wonders.

Connect to the Word

"Come to me, all you that are weary and are carrying heavy burdens, and I will give you rest. Take my yoke upon you, and learn from me; for I am gentle and humble in heart, and you will find rest for your souls. For my yoke is easy, and my burden is light."

—Matthew 11:28–30

Lesson 2: The Greatest of These Is Love

Raising a child with special needs adds stress to all areas of your life, especially your relationship as a married couple. Luckily, you don't have to go it alone. You can invite Jesus to walk with you in your marriage and transform it as he did at the wedding feast at Cana. Just as he turned water into wine when the wine had run out, allow him to replenish your love for each other.

When we think back to our wedding day, we remember that the priest asked if we would accept children lovingly from God. Children are a blessing. They bring much joy into your life, but things don't always go the way you think they will. When Danielle was born, we envisioned our beautiful little girl wearing a pink frilly tutu at ballet recitals. We imagined her in elementary school taking piano lessons and in high school learning to drive and going out on dates. We wondered what college she would attend. We thought about how beautiful she would be on her own wedding day. However, things turned out much differently. God had other plans for Danielle, which are just as beautiful and just as grand. Even though it was hard to see this at the time, we trusted in the God who knew Danielle before he formed her in her mother's womb. This trust didn't happen overnight, and sometimes our faith was sorely tested.

It's natural to experience stress when you're a parent. It comes with the territory. However, you expect that it will be infrequent and occasional. You imagine yourself finding time for the things you enjoy, for yourself and as a couple. As your children reach important childhood milestones, friends and relatives remind you to enjoy this precious time because it will be over in the blink of an eye. You anticipate the time when your life will return to normal.

So what do you do when your life doesn't return to normal, when the harsh reality of raising a child with a severe disability changes the entire structure and dynamic of your life and your marriage? The ten-plus years since Danielle was diagnosed have been very trying times for us. Not only were we dealing with the shock of having a daughter with autism, but we also suffered the loss of three of our parents in those years. There were many times when the stresses seemed too much to manage.

Looking back now, we wish someone would have been able to hand us a crystal ball so we could have seen how much progress Danielle was able to achieve by age fourteen. We wish we had trusted them when parents of older children with autism reassured us that things would get better. We once remarked to the mother of a young man with autism, who seemed so capable and competent in his late teens, that we could not imagine Danielle ever doing as well as her son. She looked at us and said in a straightforward manner, "But Danielle is only six years old. My son behaved a lot like Danielle when he was her age. He was in constant motion then just like she is now." Then she said something that seemed almost trite at the time, "You have to be patient." Looking back now, there was much merit to this. Although it wasn't apparent at the time, Danielle would make slow but steady progress, prayers would be answered, and we would witness miracles.

Now, we are able to look back and reflect on the beautiful passage read at our wedding from 1 Corinthians, Chapter 13: "Love is patient, love is kind . . . It always protects, always trusts, always hopes, always perseveres."

Now we are able to see the reason why wedding vows read the way they do, the reason why the couple promises to love each other "in good times and in bad, in sickness and in health." Like any young couple, we expected that the bad times would be few and that we would mostly have good times. However, in the early years because we were knee-deep in the experience of raising a daughter with autism, the bad times seemed to outnumber the good times. It was all too easy to miss the slow, incremental progress that was actually taking place.

Reflect on your own wedding vows and how they help you as a couple ride out the bad times. Trust that good times are already unfolding, most especially when it's hard to see that this is happening.

Identify an Appropriate Babysitter

One of the greatest challenges to marriage when your child has a disability is finding someone to watch him or her when you go out as a couple. As we mentioned, Danielle at fourteen has come a long way, and we are finding it easier to get out by ourselves. This was no easy task when she was younger. Looking back at this period when Danielle's behaviors were at their most difficult, it was really all we could do just to get through the day. We know now that we were depleted of energy, serenity, personal downtime, and time as a couple.

Start early identifying people who can give you a break and babysit. Being able to get out as a couple will help you hang in there for the long haul when things are really tough. This is something we wish we had done more often in those days. Since Danielle's behaviors could be extreme and present safety problems, we needed someone who was mature enough to handle calling Poison Control or even 911 if an emergency occurred. One of her most dangerous behaviors was putting nonedible and sometimes toxic substances into her mouth. We were always vigilant about keeping the environment clear of dangerous items, but we needed our babysitters to be able to do this as well. This called for a responsible babysitter who was at least college aged or older.

Seek small opportunities for your own self-care as a couple. This can be as simple as arranging to go to work an hour later than normal and, once the children are on the bus, picking up a gourmet coffee at a coffee shop, bringing it home, and sipping it leisurely together on the porch or at the kitchen table.

Be flexible and creative. Make accommodations that will give you time together. For instance, on our wedding anniversary one year, we were able to leave the boys and Shannon at home with a pepperoni pizza and rented movie. We took Danielle with us to a restaurant that we knew had her favorite foods on the menu. Since Danielle was busy eating, we were able to enjoy our meal and reminisce about our wedding day. We ordered dessert to celebrate. It may not have been the most romantic setting and we had Danielle with us, but she was well behaved that night and we had a lovely time. It was more important for us that the day not go unrecognized. It was clearly a case of give-and-take—we did not get out alone, but we didn't have the whole clan with us either. This arrangement, imperfect though it was, allowed us to get out and celebrate our anniversary.

Weddings are another great opportunity to go out for a fun time together. Since invitations are often sent to a couple and not to the whole family, weddings present an opportunity to hire a babysitter. As soon as you know the wedding date, start making arrangements. Consider how far from home the wedding is and how long between the ceremony and reception.

Remember to treat each invitation separately, and be flexible and realistic. We can recall being invited to several weddings over the past few years. We handled them all differently. One wedding was at our own parish. Mercedes attended the ceremony while Dave stayed home with Danielle. We did this because the babysitter wasn't available until after the ceremony was scheduled to begin. Since it was close to home, Mercedes returned after the service to pick up Dave and give final instructions to the babysitter. The two of us headed off to make the tail end of the cocktail hour and enjoy a great reception.

On another occasion we were invited to a wedding that was more than an hour away from our home. According to the invitation, there would be several hours between the wedding ceremony and the reception. At this time we were seeing a spike in some of Danielle's more negative behaviors. We are always conscious to make staying with Danielle a pleasant experience for the babysitter so that we might count on her again, and we felt more confident starting later. In this case, it made more sense for us to skip the wedding ceremony and attend the reception only.

We learned we really did need to be flexible if we wanted to get out to events like these. We had to compromise and think harder about ways we could attend while minimizing potential problems. However, we did still enjoy getting out, eating delicious meals, and dancing.

A Family Story

When our niece Jacqueline announced that she was marrying Chris, we were thrilled that he would be joining the family and so happy that all of us, including our children, were on the guest list. We knew we had to do a lot of planning in advance if we were to make the trip from New Jersey to Georgia. You're always thinking how you can make it work for your child with special needs so that in the long run it will be easier for everyone.

Transportation was our immediate concern. Traveling by plane allowed us to make the most of our limited time. The wedding was on St. Simons Island, and we looked forward to a relaxing vacation and beautiful beaches.

The wedding was lovely, and we had a wonderful time. As expected, we had to make some adaptations. This particular church had a different layout and pew configuration, which was not familiar to Danielle. We were able to sense that she was making more noise than usual and becoming more active in the pew. Maybe she would have calmed down and done okay, but we felt more comfortable and at ease with one of us taking Danielle to the back of the church and into the anteroom. Fortunately, you could still hear the entire ceremony, and if you peeked out through the glass panels of the door, it was possible to see the couple exchanging their vows.

The reception was held immediately afterward in an adjacent banquet hall with plenty of food and music. Danielle enjoyed dancing with her siblings and cousins, and we were able to get a few dances in ourselves, since so many family members were there to help. It was truly a great day. We are so glad we were able to attend, and we wish Jacqueline and Chris all of God's blessings on their marriage.

Connect to the Word

This beautiful passage from Saint Paul, read at our wedding more than twenty years ago, speaks powerfully about love, the essential ingredient in all marriages. These words grow more meaningful every day:

If I speak in the tongues of mortals and angels, but do not have love, I am a noisy gong or a clanging cymbal. And if I have prophetic powers, and understand all mysteries and all knowledge, and if I have all faith, so as to remove mountains, but do not have love, I am nothing. If I give away all my possessions, and if I hand over my body so that I may boast, but do not have love, I gain nothing.

Love is patient; love is kind; love is not envious or boastful or arrogant or rude. It does not insist on its own way; it is not irritable or resentful; it does not rejoice in wrongdoing, but rejoices in the truth. It bears all things, believes all things, hopes all things, endures all things. Love never ends.

—1 Corinthians 13:1–8

A Closing Meditation: On Love

Being deeply loved by someone gives you strength, while loving someone deeply gives you courage.

—Lao Tzu

Postscript

The day Danielle turned fifteen years old was a perfect occasion to reflect on how far she has come in her life and on how far our family has come. It had been ten years since she began formal religious education instruction. She has progressed through three sacraments: Reconciliation, Holy Eucharist, and Confirmation. Beyond making her sacraments, she has become an avid participant at Mass, following along with her picture missal and maintaining a reverent and prayerful demeanor in the pew. She crosses herself and blesses herself with holy water. She even genuflects with minor physical prompting and assistance. As an outflowing of her faith, she responds compassionately to the needs of others with a joyous countenance. Danielle is intimately involved in the rhythms of life, participating in life's celebrations and moving through grief and loss.

In light of these accomplishments, we sometimes have to remind ourselves that progress was not always easy. In fact, many times it was so difficult that we held up our hands to God and asked why he had given us a child who could not speak, why she had to endure such difficulty in her life, and why it was so hard for her and everyone in our family. Honestly, there were days when we could find no meaningful answers to such questions. Yet, days or weeks would pass, and things would start to look brighter. With prayer and persistence, Danielle and the rest of us were making gains in our development as individuals and as a family. We firmly believe that the Mass and the Sacrament of the Eucharist played a pivotal part in this growth. In fact, on Sunday mornings it is not uncommon for Danielle to go to one of her old PECS books and take out the church icon. She will hand it to us with a smile as if to say, "It is time to go to Mass now."

It's important to remember that progress in faith formation does not come overnight. It takes a lot of hard work. Parents are instrumental in this because so much of life takes place outside of formal religious education class. We are so grateful to those who volunteered their time and talents to catechize Danielle, but we also know that without active parental instruction and guidance, her religious education would not have been as successful or as complete. It takes courage and creativity for parents to develop the resources, techniques, and activities that their children need to develop a faith-filled life. We hope this book has given parents of children with special needs some direction so they can develop an individualized program that complements what parish catechists are doing.

In closing, we want to reiterate what an amazing opportunity this has been to discover the Revelation of God in our lives. We applaud the efforts of all parents of children with special needs as they struggle to live an authentic life that honors God and those in their care. We are reminded of the Letter to the Hebrews, which exhorts us to "run the race marked for you" (Hebrews 12:1).

The race is far from over, but we have at least gotten our second wind. Helen Keller once said, "I believe God has been using my life for a purpose for which I do not know, but one day I will understand and I will be satisfied." We are seeing the purpose of Danielle's life coming into sharper focus, and we believe that part of it has to do with expanding the role of people with disabilities in the life of the Church and a deepening of their faith.

Terms and Tools

American Sign Language (ASL)

Sign language is used as a form of communication by many in the autism and developmentally disabled communities.

Electronic Communication Devices and Digital Tablets

Many children with special needs use electronic communication devices and digital tablets to communicate and access information. The child presses the appropriate icons to make a sentence, which is translated into electronic speech.

Escorting

A parent, teacher, or caregiver accompanies and supports the child with prompts and reinforcement as needed.

Hand-Over-Hand Prompt

Gently place your hand over the child's hand and move it in the desired way. This prompts your child to perform an action with his or her hand such as manipulating an object, moving in a desired sequence, or pointing to the correct picture. It is an excellent way to demonstrate the desired goal or behavior when introducing a new task. Gradually fade this prompt until the child can perform the activity himself or herself. Not all children with special needs tolerate hand-over-hand prompts. They may learn to tolerate such prompts with practice and gentle handling.

Modeling

Children with special needs often respond well to modeling. This is when an adult or peer visually demonstrates the action or desired response. Some children will imitate your action in an exact manner while others may perform the action in an unusual way. They may reverse the action to correspond to their visual orientation when observing you. If this happens, instead of facing your child, stand side by side so your child sees the action from the same perspective as you do.

Pictures

Children with special needs are often very reliant on their visual sense. They may not understand language and abstract concepts but respond well to pictures and graphic displays.

Picture Icons: Picture Exchange Communication System (PECS)

Many children who are nonverbal or minimally verbal use pictures to communicate. These pictures are called icons. They are often laminated and attached to a board with Velcro depending on how they are used. They can be used to form schedules and sequence boards, and they can be used by a child to communicate and make sentences. This is known as the Picture Exchange Communication System (PECS).

Plush Tools and Other 3-D Objects

Plush figures, toys, and other 3-D objects make abstract people and concepts more concrete. They are fun to play with and manipulate, and they engage the child's tactile and kinesthetic senses. Such information may better connect with your child and help him or her learn.

Reinforcement

This means providing your child with a desired object or activity after he or she correctly performs a task or behavior. Reinforcement strengthens the chance that the child will behave in the desired fashion in similar contexts.

Role-Playing and Imaginative Play

Not all children with special needs can role-play or engage in imaginative play, but for many this can be an effective way to teach. It is fun and develops the social aspects of the faith, allowing children to experience and explore social relationships and emotions. It can also help them with problem solving.

Social Stories

These stories present events and situations that may be new, complex, or challenging. You can write your own or use stories that have been published. Typically, there is one sentence per page accompanied by a picture icon. The child is put directly into the story and referred to by his or her name. Potential problems or conflicts that might be a source of anxiety are handled in the story in the following way: "Sometimes [this] happens, but sometimes [that] happens. It's okay . . ." Reading the social story to your child helps prepare him or her for the event and may decrease any anxiety regarding ambiguity or novelty.

Resources for Parents

Sacramental Preparation and Catechesis

Adaptive Confirmation Preparation Kit for Individuals with Autism and Other Special Needs (Chicago: Loyola Press, 2014). www.loyolapress.com (Also available in Spanish)

Adaptive First Eucharist Preparation Kit for Individuals with Autism and Other Special Needs (Chicago: Loyola Press, 2012). www.loyolapress.com (Also available in Spanish)

Adaptive Reconciliation Kit for Individuals with Autism and Other Special Needs (Chicago: Loyola Press, 2012). www.loyolapress.com (Also available in Spanish)

Adaptive Finding God Program (Chicago: Loyola Press, 2015). www.loyolapress.com

Guidelines for the Celebration of the Sacraments with Persons with Disabilities (Washington, DC: United States Conference of Catholic Bishops, 1995). www.usccbpublishing.org

How to Welcome, Include, and Catechize Children with Autism and Other Special Needs: A Parish-Based Approach by Lawrence R. Sutton, Ph.D. (Chicago: Loyola Press, 2013).

National Catholic Partnership on Disability, 415 Michigan Avenue NE, Suite 95, Washington, DC 20017-4501 www.ncpd.org

Pastoral Statement of U.S. Catholic Bishops on People with Disabilities (Washington, DC: United States Conference of Catholic Bishops, 1978). www.usccbpublishing.org

Welcome and Justice for Persons with Disabilities (Washington, DC: United States Conference of Catholic Bishops, 1998). www.usccb.org

Families and Children with Special Needs
Faith, Family, and Children with Special Needs: How Catholic Parents and Their Kids with Special Needs Can Develop a Richer Spiritual Life by David Rizzo (Chicago: Loyola Press, 2012).

Manipulatives, Games, and Puzzles
Bible ABC Matching Game, www.alphabetalley.com

A Child Is Born Magnet Playset & Easter Magnet Playset, www.catholicchild.com

Jesus the Teacher, plush figure with *A Child's Bible* www.loyolapress.com/learningtools

Let's Go to Church Plush Playset, www.stjudeshop.com

My Picture Missal Flip Book and App, www.loyolapress.com/ learningtools

Plush Nativity Set, www.stjudeshop.com

Praying the Rosary Concept Kit (Loyola Press, 2015), www.loyolapress.com/learningtools

Religious Stampers, www.orientaltrading.com

SS Noah, www.catholicchild.com

Acknowledgments

We would like to thank the executive team at Loyola Press: Paul Campbell, Terry Locke, Tom McGrath, Trudy Weisel, Steve Connor, and Joellyn Cicciarelli for their commitment to publishing resources for religious education for people with special needs. We thank Maria Mondragón for her skillful editing and her kind words.

We thank Jim and Barbara Campbell and Curtis and Michaelann Martin for attending "that wedding" where the Holy Spirit brought them together and allowed our *Adaptive First Eucharist Preparation Kit* materials to land in the hands of Loyola Press. Clearly, the Holy Spirit was working that day!

We wish to thank the religious formation program at Saint Isaac Jogues Parish, especially our pastor The Very Reverend Phillip C. Pfleger; our D.R.E. Sister Clare Sabini, FMIJ; and Danielle's catechist, Grace Thoman, for always welcoming Danielle and our family and for their patience and understanding.

We wish to acknowledge and thank the many friends and family members who encouraged us.

Lastly, we acknowledge the parents of children with special needs who continue to do their best and recognize that their children are indeed "spiritually able."

About the Authors

David and Mercedes Rizzo have been married for more than twenty years and are the parents of four children. Their daughter Danielle has autism and is nonverbal. During her sacramental preparation, the lack of religious education resources available for children with severe disabilities inspired David and Mercedes, with the help of their son Brendan, to create the *Adaptive First Eucharist Preparation Kit*. They also contributed to the *Adaptive Reconciliation Kit* and the *Adaptive Confirmation Preparation Kit*. Together they have provided material for various blogs including *Catechist's Journey*, *DRE Connect*, and *Catholic Mom*. David is a physical therapist who has worked extensively with children and adults with disabilities. He is the author of *Faith, Family, and Children with Special Needs* (Loyola Press, 2012). He has presented at the Los Angeles Religious Education Congress, the Mid-Atlantic Religious Congress, The National Catholic Partnership on Disability conference, and the National Conference for Catechetical Leadership. Additionally, David has contributed to the *Finding God* series (Loyola Press). Mercedes is a certified teacher who has provided support to children with individualized education plans. She has worked in both public and parochial schools.

Also by David Rizzo

Faith, Family, and Children with Special Needs

DAVID RIZZO

David Rizzo offers hope and guidance for parents who want to help their children with disabilities grow in their spirituality and experience God in a deeper way.

Paperback | 3651-8 | $12.95

TO ORDER: Call 800.621.1008, visit loyolapress.com/store or visit your local bookseller.

Other Resources for Children with Special Needs

Everyone has the right to catechesis, which is why Loyola Press has developed these kits for individuals with autism and other special needs in English and Spanish. Preview the kits online at **www.loyolapress.com/specialneeds**.

Adaptive First Eucharist Preparation Kit

English | 3580-1 | $59.99
Spanish | 4010-2 | $59.99

Adaptive Reconciliation Kit

English | 3757-7 | $59.99
Spanish | 4011-9 | $59.99

Adaptive Confirmation Preparation Kit

English | 3877-2 | $59.99
Spanish | 4012-6 | $59.99

SAVE ON MULTIPLE KITS!

1 KIT.....................$59.99 each
2 KITS..................$49.99 each
3 KITS..................$39.99 each

The **Adaptive Learning Kits** are used successfully by people with autism, Asperger's syndrome, down syndrome, developmental disabilities, communication needs, ADD and ADHD, and learning differences.

Also Available

Jesus the Teacher Plush Figure
4460-K | $24.95

Children grow in their faith and spiritual lives in many ways. Introduce your child to prayer and the lessons of faith with this friendly plush figure of Jesus the Teacher, a Loyola Learning Tool™. Comforting and soft, this plush figure of Jesus was designed to help children connect with Our Lord while taking in his message, "I will be with you always."

Jesus the Teacher comes with a beautifully illustrated 32-page booklet titled, *A Child's Bible*. Vivid, colorful illustrations present best-loved stories from the Scriptures and introduce children to key persons from the Old and New Testaments and stories from Jesus' life on earth.

Jesus figure is 12" tall and is for children ages 4+

Read the story behind the development of the Jesus the Teacher plush figure by visiting **www.loyolapress.com/plushjesus**.